NECESSARY LIVES

NECESSARY LIVES

Biographical Reflections

B. L. REID

UNIVERSITY OF MISSOURI PRESS
COLUMBIA AND LONDON

Copyright © 1990 by
The Curators of the University of Missouri
University of Missouri Press, Columbia, Missouri 65211
Printed and bound in the United States of America
All rights reserved
5 4 3 2 1   94 93 92 91 90

Library of Congress Cataloging-in-Publication Data

Reid, B. L. (Benjamin Lawrence), 1918–
  Necessary Lives : biographical reflections
     p.   cm.
  ISBN 0-8262-0736-7 (alk. paper)
  1. English prose literature—History and criticism. 2. Authors, English—Biography—History and criticism. 3. Biography (as a literary form) 4. Autobiography. I. Title.
PR756.B56R45   1990
828'.08—dc20   89-29211
                                                         CIP

∞™ This paper meets the requirements of the
American National Standard for Permanence of Paper
for Printed Library Materials, Z39.48, 1984.

Designer: Liz Fett
Typesetter: Connell-Zeko Type & Graphics
Printer: Thomson-Shore, Inc.
Binder: Thomson-Shore, Inc.
Type face: Palatino

For Laurie and Michael

Contents

Prefatory Note ix

Acknowledgments xi

Practical Biography 1

Johnson's Life of Boswell 8

How to Die
The Example of Samuel Johnson 31

Keats and the Heart's Hornbook 45

The View from the Side 65

The House of Yeats 89

Putting in the Self
V. S. Pritchett 107

The Teller's Own Tale
The Memoirs of Frank O'Connor 126

Four Winds 142

Death of the Artist
In Memoriam, Henry Rox 159

Index 161

Prefatory Note

This book does not pretend to offer a unifying thesis or an accumulating argument. It is frankly and simply a collection, an assembling of pieces that were singly composed over the years as I worked at my long interest in biography. Such unity as the book possesses can only be that of common authorship and address to a common subject matter: biography in ramified related forms, including autobiography, memoirs, journals, letters, memorials. Everything here has already been printed at least once, and some bits, such as the first Johnson-Boswell essay, have taken on considerable antiquity. I have done little tinkering with my texts, thinking it fairer, in such a collecting, to present things essentially as they first appeared.

I thank the editors of these journals for their original approval and continuing support, and particularly for their permission to reprint:

"Practical Biography," *The Sewanee Review,* Spring 1975. Copyright 1975 by the University of the South.
"Johnson's Life of Boswell," *The Kenyon Review,* Autumn 1956.
"How to Die: The Example of Samuel Johnson," *The Sewanee Review,* Fall 1977. Copyright 1977 by the University of the South.
"Keats and the Heart's Hornbook," *The Massachusetts Review,* Spring 1961.
"The View from the Side," *The Sewanee Review,* Spring 1980. Copyright 1980 by B. L. Reid.
"The House of Yeats," *The Hudson Review,* Autumn 1965.
"Putting in the Self: V. S. Pritchett," *The Sewanee Review,* Spring 1977. Copyright 1977 by the University of the South.
"The Teller's Own Tale: The Memoirs of Frank O'Connor," *The Sewanee Review,* Winter 1976. Copyright 1976 by the University of the South.
"Four Winds," *The Sewanee Review,* Spring 1979. Copyright 1979 by B. L. Reid.
"Death of the Artist: In Memoriam, Henry Rox," *The Mount Holyoke Alumnae Quarterly,* Spring 1988.

Acknowledgments

My primary obligation here is owed to George Core, editor of the *Sewanee Review,* who is a warm veteran friend of my writing and who conceived the idea of making a book out of this selection of papers on biography.

At the University of Missouri Press, I thank Beverly Jarrett, the Director; Jane Lago, the Managing Editor, who did the basic editorial work; Liz Fett, who did the design work; and Karen Caplinger and Kathryn Conrad, who were in charge of publicity for the book. All have served me very well indeed.

Thomas Jacob of South Hadley, Massachusetts, made the jacket photograph, and I thank him as well.

NECESSARY LIVES

Practical Biography

I am concerned with the nature and function of biography and I wish to speak in part from my own experience in working at the art, or craft, or trade—whatever it is. So I hope I may be forgiven if I speak in a way that is quite personal and didactic, even dogmatic. I wish to oppose what seems the commonest, the almost universal, assumption of critics of biographical writing: that biography is a branch of the fine arts; that its ambiance and its obligations are essentially the same as those of prose fiction; that the biographer's duty like the novelist's is to entertain us with a crisp tale upon which he has imposed a sweet shapeliness, a thematic order, a modulated movement toward points of climax, a structure from which he has cut away everything not vivid and concentric. This view seems to me so wrong, and so seldom questioned, that in questioning it I feel like the little boy in the tale of the emperor's new clothes, and doubt the evidence of my own eyes.

Obviously I shall find many to refute me, and I do speak under correction. I should admit at once, too, that I do not qualify as a systematic student or theorist of biography: I have not by any means read all the major biographies or even all the major commentaries on the form. I have not, for example, read Joseph Blotner's *Faulkner*; that is another of my unfulfilled promises of last summer. But I intend to read it; I have even gone so far as to buy it. I do not find it in advance absurd that Blotner wrote over two thousand pages on Faulkner's life. I look forward to his book in the same spirit with which Tennyson read the long novels of Samuel Richardson: "I love those great still books," he said. But I shall not expect the biography to read like a novel: what I hope is that it will tell me everything not trivial that is known about William Faulkner, set down in the order of time, as it occurred in his life. That will yield what seems to me the essential biographical satisfaction.

My own credentials as a biographer are not grand and can be listed very shortly: two full-length biographies, one volume of memoirs, a dozen essays. I must tell something of my history in the biographical trade (as I prefer to call it), for my own experience lies at the base of such small theories of biography as I am ready to profess. As a young man I had written fiction and poetry, but my Muse was undependable, and when I turned for a living to an academic career my reading, talking, and writing turned naturally in the direction we call critical. It is a fairly familiar story. I was happy enough until about twenty years ago when I realized, quite suddenly, that my gorge had risen against the whole process of criticism, at least of contemporary criticism, my own as well as that of others. To read Aristotle and Johnson and Coleridge and Arnold was still a pleasure, but I found I could hardly drive myself through an essay by a contemporary, and to reread my own papers made my flesh creep. I had never been good at big formulaic thinking, but I had got pretty good at the new-critical kind of reading: I could look at a work and tell what went on in it and describe its sources of power in fairly classy language. That was a useful kind of pedagogy, but was it really a sufficiently useful kind of writing, of public discourse, to urge one to contribute to its infinite multiplication? I asked myself why I should add to the supply of a kind of writing I could hardly bear to read.

I know there was vanity in this attitude, and no doubt an element merely menopausal, but the feeling was none the less powerful. What bothered me most was that criticism seemed to be turning more and more into a set of traps for the ego. Looking at my own essays, for example, I found a good deal more of manner than of matter. I was seeing little that a reasonably intelligent graduate student could not see, and I was saying it more and more elegantly. Suddenly I could not bear my critical style any longer. I wanted to slap its jaws and wring its neck, to squeeze the unction out of it. I began working consciously at my style, trying to simplify it to the point where I could feel I was no longer overwriting—no longer swaying my leaves and flowers in the sun, in Yeats's phrase.

But I craved a deeper purgation. Still trying to understand my mood, I began to see that what was happening to me intellectually was that I was growing more and more tired of opinion and at the same time more and more interested in fact, in history. I had grown bored with criticism because it was the literary vestment of opinion, and that too often pretentious and egotistical. I am not proud of my boredom and I do not wish to recommend it to anyone else. I do not for a moment assume that good and useful criticism can no longer be written. I feel simply that criticism needs to mind its manners: to sit more often silent, and when reflection summons something original, to say it with utmost modesty. Modesty may be a queer word in the context of the present personal dogmatism. I dwell on my own experience because it is what I know and because it has been for me illustrative or monitory. I found that as I grew older I grew wearier, less patient, and drew closer to the actual with a certain homesickness. For example, I began actually to like my father-in-law, after twenty years of exasperation: I had begun to understand him as a fact, a living and formidable fact, and an interesting one.

What I seemed to need, then, was a new kind of subject matter, one oriented to fact not opinion, and one that would ask for straight exposition and not let me get away with anything but plain honest English prose. Biography was an obvious choice and I determined to have a go at it. I had always been nearly as interested in the lives of writers as in their works and had often fudged against the new-critical prohibition of the personal heresy—finding Keats's letters for example a great help in understanding the emotions of his odes, or Melville's letter to Hawthorne a help in putting names to the size and tension of *Moby-Dick*. The Irish context was another natural choice for me in that as a student and teacher I had spent a great deal of time on the modern Irish writers, on Joyce and Yeats in particular, and had been fascinated for years by the quality of life that seemed to lie behind and within those writings, their energy and their complex passionateness: bitter and gay, as Yeats named the Irish note. One could describe those qualities in the literature; but I wanted now to get at them in the life underlying: they must be a property of a culture. Could one penetrate them a bit by examining a single life or two?

Now I realized that indeed I had chosen my first subject years ago, when I had filed away in one corner of my head the baffling figure of John Quinn, who seemed to have known and served practically everybody who was anybody in the arts in the first quarter of this century. Quinn was an American Irishman, the son of immigrants, who had made good as a corporation lawyer in New York: evidently a strange subject for a literary bloke like me. But remember that I had discovered fact, and that I now liked my father-in-law. There was the fact of Quinn's strange ubiquitousness, the way he kept cropping up in useful offices in lives that mattered: he seemed to have made himself a sort of international hodman of the arts, a man who helped things happen for prime creative spirits. He paid good money for manuscripts that nobody else wanted and so came to own, for example, nearly all of Conrad's, Joyce's *Ulysses*, and Eliot's *The Waste Land* with Ezra Pound's not yet famous emendations; he bought wholesale the strange new paintings and sculptures of the School of Paris; he negotiated contracts with publishers and bought fifty at a time of new books by writers he cared about; he grubstaked

Ford and Pound and Eliot and *The Little Review;* and he knew and served all the needy Irishmen of genius. Yeats dedicated to him *The Trembling of the Veil:* "To John Quinn my friend and helper and friend and helper of certain people mentioned in this book."

When I began to work I knew this story only in barest outline. The process of filling it out, piece by piece, was for me an immense satisfaction. I spent several years in research, in the interstices of teaching, finding my facts and setting them down one at a time, each a separate pleasure. I cannot remember that any single fact bored me as I found it, though in the final proportion many had to be judged trivial and rejected in the writing. I loved the whole archaeological sensation of recovering an interesting and serviceable life, one piece at a time, of preserving it and passing it on. Isn't that the point of biography? If it is an art it is one of the useful arts. Its obligation is to the truth. Inhabiting as we all do the mysterious and painful Kingdom of This World, biography is one of the things we need. For it tells us in signal instances, illustrious or infamous, in any case exemplary, what it has meant to be human, to live a life. That seems to me biography's essential duty, its essential pleasure.

When I sat down at last to write the narrative of John Quinn's life I made a queer little discovery that came with an effect of shock and liberation: it dawned on me that biography is a form one writes in the past tense, not in the spurious present of literary criticism. What simplicity, I thought; what candor. It was then I saw what I still believe: that biography is not in its nature a fine art; it is a branch of history and Clio is its Muse. Its essence is fact and its shaper is time. As history, the history of the single life, it deals with personality in motion, with actions and events, with motives and feelings when they can be known, but all in the order of time, of sequence, the order of linked occurrence—than which nothing is more powerful and few things more interesting. Other kinds of order, the kinds that shorten and sweeten and rearrange and simplify and give the reviewers the novelistic satisfactions they all seem to crave, may please the vanity of the biographical inventor, one more artist manqué, but Clio will turn away deprived and frowning.

The main questions I wanted to ask of Quinn's life were what did he do, in what order, and what did it all add up to as a personality and a life. I felt little temptation to speculate about the unknown, or to invent and impose an order of my own: I was finding too much pleasure in the feeling that I was writing a bit of history. My final structure was unforgivingly chronological: of twenty chapters only the first and the last carried any title other than that of the simple date of the year under scrutiny. And the style I had tried to keep plain and vigorous was called in the first prominent review flatfooted. Of course I ground my teeth; but I felt that Clio was not mocked.

Of my life of Roger Casement, there is space to say little. I had enjoyed the Quinn process so keenly that I knew I wanted to try another biography, and I turned to Casement after I had been forestalled by swifter scholars on two other subjects I had marked out: John Butler Yeats, the painter-philosopher father of the poet, and George William Russell, or Æ, the poet, painter, mystic, and man of affairs who was in many ways the most interesting figure in the whole modern movement in Ireland. The context of Casement—a romantically handsome Irishman who became a British consul and a famous humanitarian before turning revolutionary patriot, conspiring with the Germans, and dying in a British hangman's noose for high treason after the Easter Rising in 1916—was even less literary than that of Quinn. "Oh, that's very political," one of my colleagues protested when he heard I was taking up Casement. But that troubled me little, as a fledgling biographer convinced that I was writing history not literature. Casement interested me precisely because none of the existing accounts made him seem real, a credible human being. The visible story was all melodrama, flickering like an old blue movie in which one could make out only a dim but striking figure doing and suffering remarkable things. The hero seemed an abstraction, only an idea of a man. Yet I was haunted by the feeling that Casement for all his strangeness really possessed representative value: that there was something classic and symptomatic about him, as an Irishman and a citizen of our troubled culture. I wanted to try to define the daily living man behind the extraordinary events.

This fascination with the quotidian is one of the habits for which biographers are regularly chided by critics, who, craving plot and dramatic tension, dismiss the daily as mere besotted inclusiveness. Yet a biographer's first duty is to recover the actual; and what is more powerful in a man's life than the detail of his days? I take real comfort and instruction in Dr. Johnson's statement to Boswell: " 'Sir, nothing is too little for so little a creature as man.' " And I confess to feeling an odd little private thrill when I found a ragged notebook that included Roger Casement's laundry list for the 12th of May in 1899 in Loanda on the west coast of Africa. I felt my nostrils flaring: I had been granted a quick intimation that seemed to be olfactory, a whiff of the real dailiness of a British consul's life in tropical parts and Victorian times. A biographer yearns to draw closer to his subject, to achieve the illusion of knowing. I did not record Casement's laundry list in my text, but I am not ashamed to say that I stuck a sample of it into a footnote.

I hope it is clear that in calling biography a mode of history rather than of literature, a useful rather than a fine art, I do not mean to set up a rigid either/or distinction, or to suggest an antipathy between the modes. I do not at all mean to say that a useful art cannot be fine, or that a fine art is not useful: I should affirm, passionately, quite the opposite. The problem is one of being true to the genius of a genre. When a biography sets out to produce the shapes and excitements of prose fiction it begins to falsify its own nature and it fails to fulfill its basic function of truthful chronicle, of the ordering of fact within the discipline of time. Certainly biography ought to be well written. I am reminded of Ezra Pound's early fiat: "Poetry ought to be at least as well written as prose." Biography ought to be as well written as a novel; but it should not try to be, or to feel like, a novel. Biography becomes a fine art when it performs superbly within the right limits of its own nature.

Biography should be decently selective rather than drudgingly inclusive: it should spare us the truly trivial. But it should not fear to find certain small things significant: "This Flemish picture," Boswell called his book, accurately and with proper fondness. The biographer should let his material form its own shapes: lives do form patterns, but patterns accumulate one piece at a time. One must be wary of the tempting "high *Priori* road," as Pope calls it: of fitting data into preconceived designs, the temptation to neaten and intensify and thereby to falsify the often disorderly order of time. Biography's strength and its integrity are ones of subject matter, of honorable and tasteful treatment of an interesting subject. Boswell's biography is still the greatest and a supremely interesting book because it treats honorably and tastefully a superb subject—probably the greatest Englishman of all and a man who had never known how to be dull.

The question of the nature of biography is by no means only aesthetic. I shall carry my assertions one stage further to say that biography is not only a useful art but a necessary one: necessary precisely because it is useful. I mean simply that human psychology, human experience is a beautiful and awful mystery and that biography is one of the few efficient lights one can carry into the labyrinth. Hence, if biography bears an obligation to history, history also bears an obligation to biography: a duty to offer itself for the telling. I should go so far as to say that every literate person who lives a notable life ought to write a memoir. When one of the masters of the form, V. S. Pritchett, lectured at my college I put that question to him: Isn't there such a thing as a duty to write an autobiography? He stared at me as if I were a bit mad; but I still think my implication was right. Can we possibly understand nineteenth-century America without *The Education of Henry Adams,* or Victorian England without Edmund Gosse's *Father and Son*? What can one say of John Keats's letters except "Thank God"? How much news of art and life moves in Yeats's *Autobiography.*

I wish very much that Eliot and Pound and Auden had written the story of their own lives. But all were adamant against it, dourly guarding what they strangely supposed was their privacy. Eliot, you remember, commanded that no biography of him was to be written; and Auden appealed to his friends to destroy their letters from him. That sort of mortmain strikes me as egotistical and wrong and in the long run pointless. It will not prevent a biography, only make it poorer, less useful. When a man makes himself a public man, it seems to me, he abandons the privilege of privacy that had been his option. Nobody requires a man to lead an interesting life in the world's eye; but my heartless biographer's feeling is that once he has done so he becomes a property of history and hence of biography. I hope no one will destroy his letters from Auden.

Johnson's Life of Boswell

"I have one of the most singular minds that ever was formed," James Boswell wrote in his journal on the eighth of February in 1768; we applaud the statement, because we have long thought the same thing, and because we feel that prodigal as he is Boswell cannot be too prodigal with such evidences of his huge confessional urge and his dumbfounded narcissism. We need all these and more to understand him. Amazed as we must be at the raveled case history of Boswell, we cannot be more amazed than Boswell himself was. Again and again his journals and letters show him wide-eyed at his own spectacle—delighted, frightened, querulous, or despairing, but always bewildered. On the eve of his departure for the continent in the summer of 1763 Boswell wrote to Sir David Dalrymple—one of the first of that series of older mentors whom he supplicated in the configuration of adolescence he never outgrew—the following ominous compound of confession, resolution, and despair:

> My great object is to attain a proper conduct in life. How sad will it be, if I turn no better than I am; I have much vivacity, which leads me to dissipation and folly. This, I think, I can restrain. But I will be moderate, and not aim at a stiff sageness and buckram correctness. I must, however, own to you, that I have at bottom a melancholy cast; which dissipation relieves by making me thoughtless, and therefore, an easier, tho' a more contemptible, animal. I dread a return of this malady. I am always apprehensive of it. . . . Tell me . . . if years do not strengthen the mind, and make it less susceptible of being hurt? and if having a rational object will not keep up my spirits?

The same confusion of motive, lighter in tone, reappears in a letter to William Temple of 1767: "My life is one of the most romantic that I believe either you or I really know of; and yet I am a very sensible, good sort of man. What is the meaning of this, Temple? You may depend upon it, that very soon my follies will be at an end, and I shall turn out an admirable member of society." In between these letters occurs one of the most pathetic of all Boswellian documents, his "Inviolable Plan, To be read over frequently," which is part of the second-person *retenu* journal of 1763–1764, in Holland. The first paragraph of this long piece, the stratagem of a man not far from collapse, shows us as nothing else can Boswell's chronic bewilderment:

> You have got an excellent heart and bright parts. You are born to a respectable station in life. You are bound to do the duties of a *Laird* of Auchinleck. For some years past you have been idle, dissipated, absurd, and unhappy. Let those years be thought of no more. You are now determined to form yourself into a man. Formerly all your resolutions were overturned by a fit of the spleen. You believed that you had a real distemper. On your first coming to Utrecht you yielded to that idea. You endured severe torment. You was pitiful and wretched. You was in danger of utter ruin. This severe shock has proved to the highest advantage. Your friend Temple showed you that idleness was your sole disease. The Rambler showed you that vacuity, gloom, and fretfulness were the causes of your woe, and that you was only afflicted as others are. He furnished you with principles of philosophy and piety to support the soul at all times. You returned to Utrecht determined. You studied with diligence. You grew quite well. This is a certain fact. You must never forget it.

For a long time, especially after Macaulay, it was fashionable to despise Boswell, and that was easy; for the past generation, after the treasure troves of Malahide and Fettercairn, it has been fashionable to "understand" Boswell, and that is not easy at all. In fact, though the despicable data are superabundant now, it is probably harder than ever either to despise or to understand this really incredible man.

Yet our feelings about Boswell are so painful and ambiguous that they will not let us rest; they push us on toward that extravagant strangeness at the heart of the man. Why did Johnson, who did not suffer fools gladly, suffer Boswell, who had so many of the traits? What was the psychology of that incongruous relationship? All of us feel the incongruity, though we feel it less violently than Macaulay, and though we will not be tempted to reduce it as Walpole did in calling it the "story of a mountebank and his zany." Macaulay's is the intellectual-snob view of the relationship. We may easily forget, too, that there was an obverse of this: the view of Boswell's Scottish circle which held that, far from "climbing" in his pursuit of Johnson, Boswell was actually condescending disgracefully. Thus "old Touchwood Auchinleck," as Carlyle called Boswell's father, scorned his son for "taking on" with "ane that keeped a schule, and ca'd it an academy"; and Margaret Boswell, as everybody knows, moved by this motive and by shame at her husband's ductility, remarked, "I have seen many a bear led by a man: but I never before saw a man led by a bear." Boswell himself felt the incongruity in the standard form and wrote to Sir David Dalrymple: "You will smile to think of the association of so enormous a genius with one so slender."

We will find it instructive to trace with some care the earliest motions of this friendship in the weeks between the first meeting on May 16, 1763, and Boswell's sailing for Holland on August 6. For what we find is that, after the first awful one-two to Boswell's wind in Davies's shop, Johnson is if anything more aggressively anxious than the younger man to form and sustain their union; finding Boswell still standing after the horrendous assault, Johnson in effect reaches out and gathers him into his arms. Here, briefly, is the sequence as it develops in Boswell's *London Journal*.

On the day after his meeting with the great moralist Boswell has an "agreeable congress" with a street girl named Alice Gibbs in a "snug place" in a London lane. On the nineteenth, at the Shakespeare's Head, he has a near miss, as "Macdonald," "a Scotch Highlander," with one woman, then scores with two: "I solaced my existence with them one after the other, according to their seniority." Next day his "blood still thrilled with pleasure"; that evening, meeting Lady Margaret Hume, with whom he had broken an engagement, "I apologized for myself by saying that I was an odd man. She seemed to understand my worth, and said it was a pity that I should just be lost in the common stream of people here." On Saturday, May 21, he drinks tea with Temple and attends Temple's lecture of that kind which he always seemed to enjoy almost as much as whoring: "Temple . . . was in fine frame and talked to me seriously of getting out of a course of dissipation and rattling and acquiring regularity and reserve, in order to attain dignity of character and happiness. He had much weight with me, and I resolved to be in earnest to pursue the course which he admired."

On Tuesday he meets three seasoned rounders, the "London Geniuses," Wilkes, Churchill, and Lloyd. "From this chorus, which was rather too outrageous and profane, I went and waited upon Mr. Samuel Johnson"—finding him "very solemn and very slovenly." Johnson treats him well and presses him to stay after other callers have left: " 'Sir,' said I, 'I am afraid that I intrude upon you. It is benevolent to allow me to sit and hear you.' He was pleased with this compliment, which I sincerely paid him, and he said he was obliged to any man who visited him. I was proud to sit in such company." There is talk of knowledge and morality. Then "he pressed me to stay a second time, which I did." Johnson sketches his own prowling habits—about the town from four in the afternoon until two in the morning. Boswell dares to wonder if this is a good use of talents, and Johnson, amazingly, accepts the censure and agrees with it. Before they part with a cordial handshake Johnson promises to visit Boswell in his lodgings. Some lines are already beginning to appear: Johnson is restless and lonely, afraid of solitude, grateful for distraction, willing to be admired; Boswell is willing to listen, willing to compliment, proud of his acquaintance, genuinely anxious for moral and intellectual buttressing. Clearly the two men are hitting it off, and gratitude is moving in both directions.

There is a good deal of rather dull sociability in these days with Boswell's worthy—too worthy—friend Temple and his younger brother Bob; but Bob shows unexpected parts when he introduces Boswell to "a Miss Temple, an exceeding pretty girl . . . kept by a man of £4,000 a year . . . very amorous, and . . . kind to her favourites without any views of interest." On Saturday, June 4, Boswell has a gaudy time celebrating the king's birthnight, dressing himself as a "complete blackguard" in his rowdiest clothes and "roaring along" through the town wenching and brawling, and much set up that in spite of his disguise he is everywhere recognized as a gentleman. Then on the thirteenth he meets Johnson again and finds him as formerly communicative and cordial. Boswell feels himself seriously edified and ennobled: "I never am with this great man without feeling myself bettered and rendered happier." Johnson takes leave of him with a handshake, bids him to call oftener and not to fear that he is troublesome, and assures Boswell that he will be very glad to see him. "Can I help being vain of this?" the young man asks his journal, very reasonably.

At the Mitre on the evening of the twenty-fifth of June their talk is the most expansive and the most personal to date. There is a random literary preamble and then Boswell, as he so loved to do, opens his heart on the subject of himself: "I then told my history to Mr. Johnson, which he listened to with attention." Boswell stresses his return to Christianity after a fling at infidelity, and Johnson, "much pleased with my ingenuous open way"—and with his own skeptical youth no doubt recalled to mind—cries, "Give me your hand. I have taken a liking to you." Johnson discourses on the Christian Evidences. Boswell then opens his heart yet further: "I told him all my story"—emphasizing, apparently, his painful squirming under his father's harsh disapprobation; for Johnson offers balm for his adolescent sense of failure (" 'Sir,' said he, 'your father has been wanting to make the man of you at twenty which you will be at thirty' ") and props for that huge but shaky ego of Boswell's ("Sir, let me tell you that to be a Scotch landlord, where you have a number of families dependent upon and attached to you, is perhaps as high a situation as humanity can arrive at"). Johnson assures him that he need feel no special pressure in forming his plan of study. Now, feeling all this big hovering warmth where before all had been so cold and unsure, Boswell makes the crucial gestures:

> I put out my hand. "Will you really take charge of me? It is very good in you, Mr. Johnson, to allow me to sit with you thus. Had I but thought some years ago that I should pass an evening with the Authour of *The Rambler!*" These expressions were all from the heart, and he perceived that they were; and he was very complacent and said, "Sir, I am glad we have met. I hope we shall pass many evenings and mornings too together."

There is a little more talk of "authours" and "perambulation," they sit until nearly two in the morning, finish two bottles of wine, and Boswell goes home "in high exultation."

On the first of July, Boswell sups with Johnson and Goldsmith at the Mitre; the literary talk is undistinguished, but Goldsmith comes out with a cardinal statement, one of those independent analyses of Boswell that we very much need to understand a part of his function for Johnson: "He said I had a method of making people speak. 'Sir,' said I, 'that is next best to speaking myself.' 'Nay,' said he, 'but you do both.' I must say indeed that if I excel in anything, it is in address and in making myself easily agreeable." Boswell concludes, complacently, "This evening passed very well, I was very quiet and attentive."

The next meeting, July 5, is of interest only because it is the occasion of the first of Boswell's disagreements with Johnson—here, as usually, silent—on matters of literary taste. But the meeting of the following day is a famous one. Boswell has engaged Johnson and others to supper at his lodgings, but this is prevented by a violent quarrel with his landlord in consequence of a noisy party in Boswell's rooms the night before. So he assembles his company at the Mitre instead—"Mr. Samuel Johnson, Dr. Goldsmith, Mr. Ogilvie, Mr. Davies, bookseller, and Mr. Eccles, an Irish gentleman of fortune." This evening is clearly the crown, socially and intellectually, of Boswell's life to date, and he is quietly proud of the figure he makes:

> I was well dressed and in excellent spirits, neither muddy nor flashy. I sat with much secret pride, thinking of my having such a company with me. I behaved with ease and propriety, and did not attempt at all to show away; but gently assisted conversation by those little arts which serve to make people throw out their sentiments with ease and freedom.

There is fine random talk of literature and politics, and then Johnson gets off his sally: "the noblest prospect that a Scotsman ever sees is the road which leads him to England." Boswell reproves, silently, Johnson's "want of taste in laughing at the wild grandeur of nature" and is moved to a—silent—fulsome apostrophe to that wild grandeur: "O Arthur Seat, thou venerable mountain!" and so on. Boswell closes his account of the evening with another bit of that self-gratulation which, in the sequel, turns so funny and so heartbreaking: "This evening I have had much pleasure. That is being truly rich. And riches are only a good because men have a pleasure in spending them, or in hoarding them up. I have received this night both instruction and pleasure."

On the fourteenth of July, Boswell and Johnson are at the Mitre again. Boswell wonders why he gets on so well with Johnson—"You and I, Sir, are very good companions"—and so poorly with his father, when the two men are of an age. Johnson lays the difference to his own cosmopolitanism as compared to the provincialism of Lord Auchinleck. Then, seeking as always the principle behind the particular, he comes up with one of the more acute of his "general truths": "Besides, there must always be a struggle between a father and son, while the one aims at power and the other at independency." Boswell passes on "some very pretty compliments, which pleased him much," from Sir David Dalrymple to Johnson. Johnson advises Boswell to keep a journal of his life, "fair and undisguised," and is glad to hear that Boswell has already done so for some time. Boswell feels a quick access of pride at having anticipated the moralist: "And now, O my journal! art thou not highly dignified? Shalt thou not flourish tenfold?" But it is clear that Johnson conceives a journal as a matter for the closet only: "He said indeed that I should keep it private, and that I might surely have a friend who would burn it in case of my death." Boswell, fortunately for us, congenitally unsympathetic to all this huddling up and secrecy, shrinks from the idea of burning: "I rather encourage the idea of having it carefully laid up among the archives of Auchinleck." When they part, after two bottles of port between them, Boswell says, "He took me cordially by the hand and said, 'My dear Boswell! I do love you very much.'"

On the nineteenth Boswell has a look at Johnson's library, with its books in dust and confusion, its "chymical" apparatus, and its scattering of manuscript leaves. Next day he invites Johnson, Dr. Blair, and Dempster to supper in his chambers. Johnson talks a great deal of hardheaded pragmatic morality, much of it on his favorite subject of "subordination." Dr. Blair leaves early and reproves "Jamie" *sotto voce* at the door: "There are few people in Edinburgh who would keep company with this man." But Boswell will have none of this, preferring the reverse snobbery with its nice distinction of himself: "sure I am there are very few people in Edinburgh with whom Mr. Johnson would keep company." Again this evening he finds his own conduct satisfactory: "I behaved extremely well tonight. I was attentive and cheerful and manly." After Johnson leaves, Boswell, full of reflected powers, continues to beat down Dempster on the issue of subordination: "He appeared to me a very weak man; and I exulted at the triumph of sound principles over sophistry."

On the evening of the twenty-second in a room at the Turk's Head, the older man offers one of the revealing analyses of the relationship:

> Mr. Johnson said he loved the acquaintance of young people. "Because," said he, "in the first place, I don't like to think myself turning old. In the next place, young acquaintances must last longest, if they do last; and in the next place, young men have more virtue than old men. They have more generous sentiments in every respect. I love the young dogs of this age: they have more wit and humour and knowledge of life than we had."

Boswell and Johnson discover yet another meeting ground, their common susceptibility to deep depression or "hypochondria." There is a pleasant interchange of symptoms. Johnson reverts, obsessively, to the subject of subordination. Then he expresses a desire to perambulate the Hebrides with Boswell, and seconds that with unusual words of kindness: "He said, 'There are few people whom I take so much to as you'; and when I talked of leaving England, he said (with an affection that almost made me cry), 'My dear Boswell! I should be very unhappy at parting, did I think we were not to meet again.'"

On the twenty-fifth Boswell tries his fledgling oratorical powers at the Robin Hood Society, with applause from the audience but little from himself: he is full of self-doubt. On the twenty-eighth he records that he has met Peggy Doig, the mother of his first illegitimate child, in town, and read her a lecture on loose behavior. That evening he and Johnson again share a room at the Turk's Head, and after some discourse of Swift and Addison the talk shifts to a more momentous subject:

> We then talked of Me. He said that I was very forward in knowledge for my age; that a man had no reason to complain who held a middle place and had many below him; and that perhaps I had not six above me. Perhaps not one. He did not know one. This was very high. I asked him, if he was my father, and if I did well at the law, if he would be pleased with me. "Sir," said he, "I should be pleased with you whatever way of life you followed, since you are now in so good a way. Time will do all that is wanting. Indeed, when you was

in the irreligious way, I should not have been pleased with you." I returned him many thanks for having established my principles.

Boswell presses for further advice on his Utrecht studies, and Johnson suggests that they "make a day" of the subject on Saturday at Greenwich. At the end of the day Boswell pauses once more to note his delight and wonderment at Johnson's continued intimacy: "It must be something curious for the people in the Turk's Head Coffee-house to see this great man and poor Me so often together by ourselves. My vanity is much flattered."

Saturday is marked first by the touching colloquy with the boat boy, so nicely highlighted in the *Life:* "He then said to the boy, 'What would you give, Sir, to know about the Argonauts?' 'Sir,' said he, 'I would give what I have.' The reply pleased Mr. Johnson much." Standing on the banks of the Thames, Boswell pulls from a strategic pocket a copy of *London: A Poem,* reads from it, then "literally" stoops to kiss the sacred ground. Johnson's specific advice on studies turns out to be sufficiently cloudy: "he run over the grand scale of human knowledge, advised me to select some particular branch to excel in, but to have a little of every kind"—a major and many minors. The day's capstone is glorious: Johnson proposes of his own accord to see the young man off for Europe. " 'I will go down with you to Harwich.' This prodigious mark of his affection filled me with gratitude and vanity." Well it might: for the sedentary, citified Johnson, here was a heroic condescension. But Johnson's largesse is not yet done; he expresses a desire to be with the young laird at Auchinleck: "I must be there, and we will live in the Old Castle; and if there is no room remaining, we will build one."

Boswell spends most of Tuesday, August 2, in Johnson's company, the forenoon in his own chambers, tea with Mrs. Williams in Bolt-court— another milestone—and supper at the Turk's Head. He has been for some days in a melancholy fit for fear of the European trial, but this evening he finds that "Mr. Johnson filled my mind with so many noble and just sentiments that the Demon of Despondency was driven away." Next evening they sup again at the same inn, but Boswell's head is so heavy from having sat up all the previous night that even Johnson can barely keep him awake.

The *London Journal* closes on this sleepy note, and for an account of the last of these great days we must turn to the *Life.* The two men take coach for Harwich in the early morning of August 5. For our purposes the only significant passage of the journey is Johnson's open guying of Boswell before his fellow passengers as a young man who has already been idle in Edinburgh, Glasgow, and London and is now going off to be idle in Utrecht. Boswell shows himself rather pained. Before they retire for the night at Colchester, Johnson resumes his guying, borrowing a metaphor from a moth which has just burnt itself in their candle flame to chide Boswell for "fanciful apprehension of unhappiness": "That creature was its own tormentor, and I believe its name was Boswell." Next day Johnson performs his famous athletic refutation of Berkeley by kicking the stone outside the church in Harwich: "I refute it *thus*." This sets the stage with a nice emphasis for the closing scene:

> My reverend friend walked down with me to the beach, where we embraced and parted with tenderness, and engaged to correspond by letters. I said, "I hope, Sir, you will not forget me in my absence."
>
> JOHNSON. "Nay, Sir, it is more likely you should forget me, than that I should forget you." As the vessel put out to sea, I kept my eyes upon him for a considerable time, while he remained rolling his majestick frame in his usual manner: and at last I perceived him walk back into the town, and he disappeared.

So ends the first phase of the amazing friendship, and it is time to stop and take stock. These first weeks have been definitive. Our quick purview suggests matter for a number of hypotheses as to what has essentially taken place; later we may go on to test these hypotheses in the larger scene of the ensuing twenty years. One conviction that has already moved beyond hypothesis into certainty is that Boswell did not arrogantly impose himself upon an unwilling Johnson, as the cliché has long held: it is perfectly clear that, for reasons which we must determine, Boswell's company was at least as welcome to Johnson as Johnson's was to Boswell. Handshakes, embraces, and repeated overt acts and spoken assurances, most of them unsolicited, show us that beyond doubt.

Why was Boswell welcome? Much of the answer lies in the peculiarities of the Johnsonian psyche, but in conjunction with the peculiarities of the interval in which the young man made his appearance. For Boswell came to Johnson in the year after the crown pension of three hundred pounds had set him permanently free of his besetting fear of poverty, free of the need to accept any more of the onerous hackwork that had kept him alive thus far, and free thereby to indulge expansively his three most notable personal traits—his love of indolence, his love of talk, and his fear of loneliness. Boswell, with his endless willingness to sit, to saunter, and to listen, answered perfectly to all three. He had arrived at precisely the time when Johnson, who "loved to fold his legs and have out his talk," was secure at last to do so. *"Amici fures temporis,"* Johnson quotes at one time: "Friends are the thieves of time"; after 1763 Johnson wanted his time stolen, and Boswell was a patient and cunning thief.

But Boswell had ability to match his presumptuousness. Johnson's case was not so desperate that he must devote long hours to any tiresome man. Boswell was, quite simply, a genius of social intercourse. "A very *clubable* man," Johnson was to call him later; and we have seen Goldsmith's encomium. Adam Smith praised his "facility of manner," and Burke, Reynolds, and even Mrs. Thrale noted the same virtue. His sociable behavior may have been his supreme creative act. Boswell was not merely an enormous ear, as we sometimes feel in the *Life,* or a question-machine, as we feel at other times; he was a really brilliant social catalyst, one who could make others precipitate and decant the pleasurable talk that was in them, a master of "those little arts which serve to make people throw out their sentiments with ease and freedom." Johnson, who loved to talk but required it to be elicited, placed a just value on Boswell's graceful art. And Boswell could talk himself; he was not a fool and he was not dumb. Goldsmith has phrased the matter for us: " 'Nay,' said he, 'but you do both.' " Boswell, let us say, had come to the right place at the right time with the right equipment.

The discrepancy in the ages of the two men is responsible for much of the seeming incongruity of the union, but also for much of its special intimate warmth. Boswell was twenty-three, Johnson fifty-three: one thinks at once, Johnson was old enough to be his father. Exactly, Boswell and Johnson think so too: it is a note that recurs often. That Boswell sought a father-substitute in the older man is a commonplace and accurate observation. He was in flight all his life from the father Lord Auchinleck insisted on being and in search of the father Lord Auchinleck refused to be. His list is long: Lord Kames, David Hume, Sir Alexander Dick, Sir David Dalrymple, General Paoli, Sir John Pringle, Voltaire, Rousseau—and Johnson; Boswell's most significant friendships are with men of this generation, and he always approached them filially. And it is touching to find him putting to Temple, his closest confidant of his own age, the same wistful question he asked of Johnson: "Temple, if I was your son, would you be pleas'd with me?" It seems to me almost equally clear that Johnson sought in Boswell the son he had never had. That he took pleasure, vicariously, in the spectacle of youth he explicitly tells us: "I love the young dogs of this age"; and his obsessive fear of death was calmed a bit by the young vitality around him: "I don't like to think myself turning old." He felt a real kindness in a young man's eagerness for his company. Johnson's posture to Boswell is more fatherly than it is anything else—in its indulgence, its concern to teach, its affectionateness, and in the sadness of its ultimate disappointment. Johnson and Boswell anticipate, stiffly, the wry comedy of Leopold Bloom and Stephen Dedalus.

Boswell, then, played the son's part nicely by asking Johnson to be the things that, at least for the time, he took pleasure in being—confessor, moral guide, intellectual mentor, disciplinarian: the configuration of the Compleat Father. Other motives, too, there are in abundance, less interesting and on the whole less worthy: such shared crotchets as superstitiousness and hypochondria; Boswell's desire for distinction and Johnson's power and willingness to confer it; Johnson's fondness for flattery and Boswell's ability to confer it; Boswell's need as a spectacular sinner to be saved and Johnson's evangelical desire to save him. But the crucial motives of the union are the confessed social relationship and the half-confessed familial one.

There are texts which show that Johnson's regard did not cease when Boswell went abroad. As the years passed the feeling warmed at times to love, rose at times to respect, and became complicated at last by an impatience close to disgust at Boswell's habits; yet it never altered in a degree that we can call radical. The second of his letters to Boswell on the continent testifies convincingly to his undiminished affection in January 1766:

> nothing has lessened either the esteem or love with which I dismissed you at Harwich. Both have been increased by all that I have been told of you by yourself or others; and when you return, you will return to an unaltered, and, I hope, unalterable friend. . . . I long to see you, and to hear you; and hope that we shall not be so long separated again.

Just before the Scotch tour Johnson sends a brief note reproving Boswell's fulsomeness but concluding, "Think only when you see me, that you see a man who loves you, and is proud and glad that you love him."

Two years later the expression, though qualified as the later letters tend to be by distaste for Boswell's anxiousness and a progressive despair at his morals, is still one of fundamentally unshaken affection:

> Never, my dear Sir, do you take it into your head to think that I do not love you; you may settle yourself in full confidence both of my love and my esteem; I love you as a kind man, I value you as a worthy man, and I hope in time to reverence you as a man of exemplary piety. I hold you, as Hamlet has it, "in my heart of hearts."

Near the end of Boswell's annual visit in 1777 Johnson speaks to him in the same vein, wearied by his pleas for reassurance but still unequivocally willing to supply it: "My regard for you is greater almost than I have words to express; but I do not choose to be always repeating it; write it down in the first leaf of your pocket-book, and never doubt of it again." In the spring of the year before Johnson's death Boswell finds him ill at Mrs. Thrale's, applies the balm of his good company, and is told that his presence is as grateful as ever: "You must be as much with me as you can. You have done me good. You cannot think how much better I am since you came in." This is twenty years after the first meeting.

Now, if Johnson's words alone are not enough to make our point, we may adduce his actions—a quick catalog of his embraces: "He embraced me cordially"; "I went with him to his door where he embraced me and blessed me"; "He embraced me and said, 'Fare you well. God bless you for Jesus Christ's sake'"; "He took me in his arms, and said with solemn fervour, 'God bless you for Jesus Christ's sake'"; "he hug'd you to him like a sack, and grumbl'd, 'I hope we shall pass many years of regard together'"; "He took me all in his arms and kist me on both sides of the head." Even after we have discounted for eighteenth-century fervency, we have to say that these are testaments of a deep and constant tenderness.

It would be foolish to argue that the relationship had in no way decayed with the passage of time; but the essential decay, it seems to me, occurred not in Johnson's love but in the fibers of Boswell the man. Long before Johnson's death in 1784 Boswell was firmly fixed in the syndrome of inner and outer failure, and that radical slackness, though we scarcely feel it in the *Life*, had loosened and dulled, not his love or Johnson's, but Boswell's basic hold on life, his zeal and his energy, his power to keep that love the warm and active thing it began by being.

When Boswell first called at his chambers, we remember, Johnson said to him, "Sir, I am obliged to any man who visits me"; and near the end of the *Life* Boswell recalls this late tribute: "Boswell, I think I am easier with you than with almost any body." In those two brief statements, I suspect, lies the simple secret of Boswell's value to Johnson: the first expressing, in addition to a perfunctory courtesy, Johnson's almost pathetic need for the constant distraction of human company; the second expressing a quiet gratitude for the special kind of company Boswell so faithfully provided. It was on the basis of such a need on Johnson's part and such an endowment on Boswell's part that Johnson was moved to say, as Dudley Long reported, "Sir, if I were to lose Boswell, it would be like a limb amputated."

If Johnson were ever going to depreciate Boswell it would be, one suspects, to Mrs. Thrale—considering the terms of his intimacy with her, and considering the rivalry between his "Mistress" and his Boswell. Thus it is illuminating to follow a series of brief references to Boswell in a group of letters to Mrs. Thrale from Ashbourne in the fall of 1777. Note that every reference is open and approving: On September 13 he writes, "Boswell, I believe, is coming . . . I shall be glad to see him." On the fifteenth, "Last night came Boswell. I am glad that he is come. He seems to be very brisk and lively." On the eighteenth, "Boswell is with us in good humour; and plays his part with his usual vivacity." (On this the saturnine Baretti comments, "That is, he makes more noise than anybody in company, talking and laughing loud.") On the twenty-fifth Johnson closes the episode, "Boswell is gone. . . . He has been gay and good-humored in his usual way." (Baretti sneers, "That is, in his noisy and silly way.") When Boswell himself came to read Johnson's letters in Mrs. Thrale's edition in 1788 he reacted with a sense of shock and deep disenchantment—deeper than we, lacking Boswell's lofty expectations, can find strictly logical. His response is, in fact, a clear indication both of his waspish animosity to Mrs. Thrale and of the sad late confusions of his mind, and we should read it now for such evidences.

> I was disappointed a good deal, both in finding less able and less brilliant writing than I expected, and in having a proof of his fawning on a woman whom he did not esteem, because he had luxurious living in her husband's house; and in order that this fawning might not be counteracted, treating me and other friends much more lightly than we had reason to expect. This publication cooled my warmth of enthusiasm for "my illustrious friend" a good deal. I felt myself degraded from the consequence of an ancient Baron to the state of an humble attendant on an Authour; and what vexed me, thought that my collecting so much of his conversation had made the World shun me as a dangerous companion.

His complaint is not wholly lacking in justice: Johnson's letters are far less brilliant than one has a right to expect—but Johnson hated to write letters; Boswell's assiduousness in "collecting" and his candor in publishing had indeed closed doors to him, inevitably—but his own dissoluteness had closed more; Johnson's references to Boswell in his letters are indeed less eulogistic than his references elsewhere—yet only once or twice does he express himself in a way that we or Boswell could call deprecatory or patronizing. After Mrs. Thrale had read the manuscript which was to become the *Journal of a Tour to the Hebrides*, Johnson wrote to her, "You never told me, and I omitted to enquire, how you were entertained by Boswell's Journal. One would think the man had been hired to be a spy upon me." The problem of interpretation there is one of tone; Johnson may have been simply commenting, with light irony, upon Boswell's industry, as the succeeding sentence in fact suggests: "He was very diligent, and caught opportunities of writing from time to time." A more genuinely patronizing reference occurs in a letter written near the end of the Scotch tour; ironically, Johnson probably meant this as his handsomest compliment to Boswell in all the letters: "Boswell will praise my resolution and perseverance; and I shall in return celebrate his good humour and perpetual cheerfulness. He has better faculties than I had imagined; more justness of discernment; and more fecundity of images." "Than I had imagined" does suggest a curious illumination after ten years' acquaintance; it suggests that Johnson had held Boswell's serious parts in a rather light estimate all that time, and that now he suddenly realizes he has long undervalued that side of him.

Johnson never tired of Boswell as a companion of his travels—surely one of the most acid tests of friendship. He makes this repeatedly clear. There is the formal tribute in the first paragraph of his *Journey to the Western Islands of Scotland:* "finding in Mr. Boswell a companion, whose acuteness would help my inquiry, and whose gaiety of conversation and civility of manners are sufficient to counteract the inconveniences of travel, in countries less hospitable than we have passed." But more telling is such an unstudied statement as the following—made eleven years after the tour and only a few months before his death: "Boswell has a great mind to draw me to Lichfield, and as I love to travel with him, I have a mind to be drawn." To Mrs. Knowles he phrased the same judgment in terms of superlatives: "If you knew his merit as well as I do, you would say a great deal; he is the best travelling companion in the world." Finally, it is suggestive to compare the pleasure Johnson found with Boswell in Scotland with his dyspepsia on the continental tour with the Thrales.

Happily Boswell has left us a vignette in his *Journal of a Tour to the Hebrides* that shows us pretty precisely what were his services as a traveling companion to Johnson. He is both expert steward and unobtrusive master of the revels:

> I must take some credit from my assiduous attention to him, and the happy art which I have of contriving that he shall be easy wherever he goes, that he shall not be asked twice to eat or drink anything (which always disgusts him), that he shall be provided with water at his meals, and many such little things, which, if not attended to, would fret him. I have also an admirable talent of leading the conversation: I do not mean leading as in an orchestra, by playing the first fiddle, but leading as one does in examining a witness:

starting topics, and making the company pursue them. Mr. Johnson appeared to me like a great mill, into which a subject is thrown to be ground. That is the test of a subject. But indeed it requires fertile minds to furnish materials for this mill.

And near the end of the tour he gives us a scrap of action from a Glasgow scene which dramatizes the whole relationship in a flash:

I, having a letter to write, left my fellow-traveller with Messieurs Foulis. Though good and ingenious men, they had that unsettled speculative mode of conversation which is offensive to a man regularly taught at an English school and university. I found that instead of listening to the dictates of the sage, they had teased him with questions and doubtful disputations. He came in a flutter to me and desired I might come back again, for he could not bear these men. "O ho! sir," said I, "you are flying to me for refuge;" . . . He answered, with quick vivacity, "It is of two evils choosing the least." I was delighted with this flash bursting from the cloud which hung upon his mind, closed my letter directly, and joined the company.

Which is another useful dash of salt in the pudding I continue to make unnaturally sweet.

We need to turn at last to the less happy portions of the story and to fill out the picture of Johnson as Compleat Father. In one of his letters to Temple, Boswell offers a bit of ingenuousness, both pathetic and delightful, which can stand as a tentative microcosm of this history: "He is to buy for me a chest of books of his chusing off stalls, and I am to read more and drink less." Johnson sent the books, and when Boswell got around to opening them weeks later he scorned them as "a numerous and miscellaneous *Stall Library*, thrown together at random"; he then proceeded to read less and drink more. The fact is, if we tabulate Johnson's paternal utterances, his advice, his censure, and his approbation, we soon see that whereas he never ceased to love Boswell as a partner in talk or travels, he found little to approve in twenty years' experience of Boswell as son and pupil. We know perfectly well why this was true: there was little for anyone to approve in Boswell's life outside his wonderful service as Good Fellow. It is only too well known, on the testimony of the *Life* and the *Boswell Papers*, that Johnson made a parlor sport out of "tossing" Boswell, as the latter called it. But that is not very important: Johnson was only a little fonder of tossing Boswell than of tossing anyone else, and Boswell was temperamentally and philosophically very well able to bear it. He put the matter in what is after all a very just perspective:

Speaking of Mr. Johnson's roughness to me at times I told her [Mrs. Stuart] that he said to me at Edinburgh, before Dr. Blair and some more, that he reckoned the day on which he and I became acquainted one of the happiest days of his life. "Now," said I, "what a number of little attacks will it take to counterbalance this. If he gives me a hundred thousand pounds, and he takes from me a shilling, or even a guinea, now and then, what a time will it take before he gets his great gift back again." "Nay," said she, "he never can take it from you."

We need not take it much more seriously than Boswell does when Johnson regrets that Boswell had not been available for the *Dunciad* or advises him to get his head "fumigated." In the scale of the hundred-thousand-pound praise such peckish insult or bearish wit, in moments of passing pique or petty tyrannizing, makes little organic difference. What we rather want to know is how Johnson thought of Boswell when he was working most seriously at the subject.

We have the magnificent letter that Johnson wrote to Boswell in Utrecht in December 1763. Everything that follows is, sadly, a footnote to that letter, and on a descending scale moving toward weariness or despair—not so much recorded in overt statement as implied in perfunctory phrase or merely formal tone. We can follow this progress, but we need first to recall that august document, the Utrecht letter. Johnson is responding to two letters of Boswell's, the first of which especially had been a long whine of fear and discontent. Having now Boswell's continental journal, we see his actual shivering misery, something very close to madness, and it is a good deal easier for us to forgive his moaning abjectness than it can have been for Johnson. After noticing Boswell's first letter in phrases of dignified contempt—"The first, indeed, gave me an account so hopeless of the state of your mind, that it hardly admitted or deserved an answer"—Johnson then settles in an attitude that mingles austere kindness and elevated counsel in one of the most imposing things ever to come from his pen. The easy rein with which Johnson had promised to ride in those days in London has visibly tightened; the new counsel, while it is not much more specific, is vastly more stringent. The letter should be reread in any case; but perhaps one passage near the close can sufficiently suggest its tone and tenor:

> Let all such fancies, illusive and destructive, be banished henceforward from your thoughts for ever. Resolve, and keep your resolution; choose, and pursue your choice. If you spend this day in study, you will find yourself still more able to study tomorrow; not that you are to expect that you shall at once obtain a complete victory. Depravity is not very easily overcome. Resolution will sometimes relax, and diligence will sometimes be interrupted; but let no accidental surprise or deviation, whether short or long, dispose you to despondency. Consider these failings as incident to all mankind. Begin again

where you left off, and endeavour to avoid the seducements that prevailed over you before.

Johnson's strictures on Boswell's social behavior are among his shallower rebukes, and we can dispose of those fairly quickly. Society meant for Johnson basically conversation, and by the nice distinction he draws between conversation and "talk" we know well enough what were his expectations in social intercourse: "No, Sir; we had *talk* enough, but no *conversation;* there was nothing *discussed.*" There were, of course, the interdicted subjects, such as America, or "bawdy," or death. But three habits in conversation were anathema to Johnson, and he found Boswell on occasion guilty of all three: excessive use of personal applications, excessive use of a question-and-answer form, and excessive or self-conscious bookishness, especially to cover a poverty of original ideas. At one point he was moved to compliment Boswell by saying, "You and I do not talk from books." But Boswell's sin on this head was poverty rather than excess, and on another occasion Johnson called attention to his inadequate bookish foundation in general truth: "Said Mr. Johnson: 'I wish you had read more books. The foundations must be laid by reading. General principles must be had from books.'" Johnson's distaste for personal references was partly philosophical, partly temperamental: he sought principles larger than personalities, and he objected to having himself made a datum in any demonstration. The strength of his feeling about this is shown by the strength of his rebukes:

> "Sir, you put an end to all argument when you introduce your opponent himself. Have you no better manners? There is *your want.*"

> "You have but two topicks, yourself and me, and I'm sick of both. Who of our club talks of me thus, makes me a constant topick?"

His dislike for repeated questioning was equally violent. When Boswell has been too persistent Johnson says to him, "This now is such stuff as I used to talk to my mother, when I first began to think myself a clever fellow; and she ought to have whipt me for it." And again: "I will not be put to the *question.* Don't you consider, Sir, that these are not the manners of a gentleman? I will not be baited with *what* and *why;* what is this? what is that? why is a cow's tail long? why is a fox's tail bushy?" Langton told Boswell privately that Johnson had said to him, "When Boswell gets wine, his conversation consists all of questions," and this is a statement which carries us neatly from his venial to his mortal sins.

Toward Boswell's drinking and his whoring Johnson sometimes displayed a kind of easygoing complacency that is rather surprising. Boswell showed his own moral fibers at their slackest in seeking to manipulate Johnson so as to secure from him pronouncements which could be rationalized as palliative if not approving. He was perfectly sensible of the irony of his own behavior when a professed follower of the Rambler. As he says to himself en route to Ashbourne to meet the great moralist in 1777, after dallying with the chambermaids of three successive wayside inns, " 'How inconsistent,' thought I, 'is it for me to be making a pilgrimage to see Dr. Johnson, and licentiously loving wenches by the way.' " But Johnson could, as I say, respond very lightly to such peccadilloes. One of the most delightful exchanges in the *Life* is that with Wilkes which takes place on the scene of Boswell's greatest social coup, the fabulous dinner at Dilly's in 1776:

> JOHNSON. (to Mr. Wilkes) "You must know, Sir, I lately took my friend Boswell and shewed him genuine civilised life in an English provincial town. I turned him loose at Lichfield, my native city, that he might see for once real civility: for you know he lives among savages in Scotland, and among rakes in London." WILKES. "Except when he is with grave, sober, decent people like you and me." JOHNSON. (smiling) "And we ashamed of him."

Boswell's drinking is a considerable problem on the Scottish tour. He helps make way with four bowls of punch at Coirechatachan, falls into bed at five in the morning, and awakes at noon with a bursting head and shame at his unseemly course: "I thought it very inconsistent with the conduct which I ought to maintain while the companion of the Rambler." Yet Johnson is only indulgently sardonic:

> "What, drunk yet?" His tone of voice was not that of severe upbraiding; so I was relieved a little. "Sir," said I, "they kept me up." He answered, "No, you kept them up, you drunken dog." This he said with good-humoured English pleasantry. Soon afterwards, Coirechatachan, Coll, and other friends assembled around my bed. Corry had a brandy bottle and glass with him, and insisted I should take a dram. "Ay," said Dr. Johnson, "fill him drunk again. Do it in the morning that we may laugh at him all day. It is a poor thing for a fellow to get drunk at night, and skulk to bed, and let his friends have no sport." Finding him thus jocular, I became quite easy. . . . When I rose, I went into Dr. Johnson's room, and taking up Mrs. Mackinnon's prayer book, I opened it at the twentieth Sunday after Trinity, in the epistle for which I read, "And be not drunk with wine, wherein there is excess." Some would have taken this as a divine interposition.

Later in the tour Johnson faces the matter a good deal more dourly: "Mr. Johnson . . . very justly reproved me for taking the *scalck* or dram every morning. He said, 'For shame!' and that it was now really become serious. It was lucky that he corrected me." And later still we see the thing grown into a formula, with Johnson pessimistically admonitory and Boswell skulking but resolved to have his liquor:

> Another bowl was made. Mr. Johnson had gone to bed as the first was finished, and had admonished me, "Don't drink any more *poonch*." I must own that I was resolved to drink more, for I was by this time a good deal intoxicated; and I gave no answer, and slunk away from him, with a consciousness of my being brutish and yet a determination to go somewhat deeper. What I might have done I know not. But luckily before I had tasted the second bowl, I grew very sick, and was forced to perform the operation that Antony did in the Senate house, if Cicero is to be credited.

I am afraid that this is nearer to the norm of things. That Johnson was doomed to fail in his effort to reform Boswell the drunkard shows clearly in this journal entry for April 15, 1772: Boswell asks, "Would you not, Sir, allow a man oppressed with care to drink, and make himself merry?"; Johnson replies, "Yes, if he sat next *you*." Boswell, unshaken, babbles on: "I never was disturbed. I know Mr. Johnson so well, and delight in his grand explosions, even when directed against myself, so much, that I am not at all hurt." That Johnson understood the psychology and the classic pattern of the self-dramatizing drunk is clear from a passage such as this in Boswell's journal:

> HE. ". . . What hinders your reformation is that you are always speaking of it: 'General Paoli took my promise, and Dr. Johnson approves.' Now consider that nobody really cares, only they want a topick for conversation. No. Go to Scotland, and say, simply, 'I've left off wine.'" (Thrale had told him I said I had been drunk 12 times since I came to London.) I was humbled.

One other brief note from the 1776 visit suggests that whereas he understood the outlines of Boswell's case, Johnson probably had not seen all his symptoms in full flower: "He bid me divert melancholy by every means but drinking. I thought then of women, but no doubt he no more thought of my indulging in licentious copulation than of my stealing." Boswell was all his life a man in frantic flight from recurrent grinding depression, melancholia, or "hypochondria"—the "English malady" in virulent form. His escape he sought by three main routes: alcohol, women, and the company of the intellectual great. He could not do without any of the three, yet he could not bear the thought that his vices, women and wine, must sooner or later deny him his virtue, the cultivation of intelligence; so of course he tried to travel his three routes concurrently, and to deceive Johnson adequately while doing so. Thus it is significant that there are relatively so few recorded pronouncements by

Johnson on the subject of Boswell's profligacy. Either Boswell has suppressed some of Johnson's utterances—which would be very unlike him—or else he somehow managed to hide from Johnson the full heroic proportions of his sinning. If Boswell could believe after thirteen years' acquaintance that Johnson still did not know of his habitual whoring, then it seems likely that he had indeed been both lucky and successful in shielding himself from the full baleful glare of Johnson's eye. We know of his repeated vinous indiscretions in Johnson's company; yet he seems to have stopped those always short of the displays of wallowing disgracefulness which were part of his symptomatology at its lowest depths. Boswell's compulsive sexuality is a gaudy sight to the reader of his journals, but Johnson did not read those. Yet Boswell was constantly begging Johnson for palliative opinions—in the abstract—of "fornication" and "concubinage." And there is one suggestive lacuna in volume 11 of the *Boswell Papers* which indicates, as an editorial note hazards, that he may on one occasion have braved the Rambler's full wrath—and received it. On Good Friday and Easter Day—he was not one to brood about proprieties—he was steering the talk persistently in the direction of these favorite subjects; but ten pages, containing the Johnsonian record for Sunday and the complete record for Monday and Tuesday, are torn from the journal, and when it resumes the entry indicates that an explosion of some size has taken place. Perhaps April 7, 1776, was the day Boswell got what was coming to him; had he dared something like a full confession on that day?

In any case, Johnson's increasingly serious view of Boswell's dissipations is already clear; as time passed his response hardened and dulled into sadness, boredom, and disillusionment. He grew more and more hopeless of doing anything about the decaying man, and less and less willing to be troubled with his sick complaints, usually centering about his miserable melancholy. Johnson seems to have grouped Boswell's sins of depression and profligacy under the single inclusive head of failure of manliness; his diagnosis was probably accurate clinically if not terminologically. For Boswell's failures really were those of anachronism—perpetuating the fears and the susceptibilities of adolescence into manhood. "You are longer a boy than others," Johnson told him during the tour, meaning only a passing reproof; we can accept it as the richest possible text.

Johnson's disenchantment parallels, as we now know, the slow collapse of Boswell himself. On June 20, 1771, when Boswell was still relatively prelapsarian, Johnson could find grounds as yet for guarded congratulation, but he hedged that about with apprehensive good counsel:

> I never was so much pleased as now with your account of yourself; and sincerely hope, that between publick business, improving studies, and domestick pleasures, neither melancholy nor caprice will find any place for entrance. . . . My dear Sir, mind your studies, mind your business, make your lady happy, and be a good Christian.

By 1779, replying to one of Boswell's *"black dog"* letters from Scotland, Johnson is showing a firmly established impatience:

> I wish you to get rid of all intellectual excesses, and neither to exalt your pleasures, nor aggravate your vexations, beyond their real and natural state. Why should you not be as happy at Edinburgh as at Chester? *In culpa est animus, qui se non effugit usquam.* Please yourself with your wife and children, and studies, and practice.

By the summer of 1782 things were definitely going to pieces. Following the death of his father, Boswell wrote of his desire to come to London for Johnson's advice but complaining that his economy was in such a bad way that he could not afford the trip; to this Johnson's reply is abrupt and for the first time almost wholly without kindness:

> I am sorry to find, what your solicitation seems to imply, that you have already gone the whole length of your credit. This is to set the quiet of your whole life at hazard. . . . Live on what you have; live if you can on less; do not borrow either for vanity or pleasure; the vanity will end in shame, and the pleasure in regret: stay therefore at home, till you have saved money for your journey hither.

A recurrent theme in these later letters is admonition to Boswell to value and guard his wife, whose importance to him Johnson understood better than did Boswell himself: "I hope that dear Mrs. Boswell will surmount her complaints; in losing her you would lose your anchor, and be tost, without stability, by the waves of life." Upon this passage Boswell added, years later, a blubbering footnote, "The Truth of this has been proved by sad experience." As he nears his own end, Johnson's tone grows more and more acid:

> Like all other men who have great friends, you begin to feel the pangs of neglected merit; and all the comfort that I can give you is, by telling you that you have probably more pangs to feel, and more neglect to suffer. You have, indeed, begun to complain too soon; and I hope I am the only confidant of your discontent. . . . Of the exaltations and depressions of

your mind you delight to talk, and I hate to hear. Drive all such fancies from you.

Still, it is very pleasant to find that two of his last letters, written in the summer before his death, while they continue to reprimand, also decisively return the balance toward kindness. Thus,

> Write to me often, and write like a man. I consider your fidelity and tenderness as a great part of the comforts which are left me, and sincerely wish we could be nearer to each other. . . . Love me as well as you can.

> Go steadily forward with lawful business or honest diversion. . . . This may seem but an ill return for your tenderness; but I mean it well, for I love you with great ardour and sincerity.

The rest of the story is famous and sad. Half of James Boswell died with Samuel Johnson in 1784 and the other half died with Margaret Montgomerie Boswell in 1789. Boswell had a way of falling into halves. What reeled on to 1795 was a husk of a man. Lord Auchinleck pressed the life from his son and when he had hollowed him out sent him into the world to be filled and propped, chemically, by alcohol and, psychologically, by men and women who had strength to spare. "I am quite restored by him," Boswell said of Johnson to Mrs. Thrale, "by transfusion of Mind." After the death of his wife he wrote to Temple, "I am the most helpless of human beings." Edmund Malone propped the husk long enough for it to patch together, with the shreds of its genius, one of the world's great books. "Let me not *think* at present," Boswell wrote to Temple during that process; "far less *resolve*. The *Life of Johnson* still keeps me up. I *must* bring that forth, and then I think I may bury myself in London, in total obscure indifference." But the husk staggered back to Scotland and got itself buried there at last, after a course of events really too painful to record.

"You are longer a boy than others," Johnson told him. Old Auchinleck gave him his congenital wound: by refusing to let him be a boy when he was young he made him a boy when he was old. The boy of thirty-five who could write, "I must really get Mr. Johnson to put me down a short, clear system of Religion," could never grow up.

Whatever shame is due Boswell for his part in the life of Boswell, very little shame is due him for his part in the life of Johnson. The self of Boswell that served Johnson served him magnificently. Johnson required him to be a superb companion, and Boswell responded with a superb performance. "I believe Mr. Boswell will be at last your best Physician," Mrs. Thrale wrote Johnson in 1773—when he thought he was going mad. Reynolds writing to Langton of Boswell in 1782 quoted Burke's opinion: "he is by much the most agreeable man he ever saw in his life." Johnson thought so too. It seems to me foolish and sentimental to overpraise Boswell. As the Compleat Son he was a heartbreaking, vicious failure. But as gay, vivid, articulate companion of the bosom, he justified Johnson in saying, as he did say, "I do love thee. I do love thee."

How to Die

The Example of Samuel Johnson

Being a sort of sermon, this exercise can logically begin with a text and an anecdote. My text I take from number 32 of the *Rambler:* "There is some reason for questioning whether the body and mind are not so proportioned, that the one can bear all which can be inflicted on the other; whether virtue cannot stand its ground as long as life, and whether a soul well principled, will not be sooner separated than subdued." The anecdote, along with most of my matter, I take from Boswell. We need to imagine a schoolboy of six or seven years, a chubby pockmarked myopic figure:

> One day, when the servant who used to be sent to school to conduct him home, had not come in time, he set out by himself, though he was then so near-sighted, that he was obliged to stoop down on his hands and knees to take a view of the kennel before he ventured to step over it. His schoolmistress, afraid that he might miss his way, or fall into the kennel, or be run over by a cart, followed him at some distance. He happened to turn about and perceive her. Feeling her careful attention as an insult to his manliness, he ran back to her in a rage, and beat her, as well as his strength would permit.

Boswell tells the story as an early illustration of "that jealous independence of spirit and impetuosity of temper, which never forsook him."

The courage of Samuel Johnson took many forms, including, obviously, the pugnacious. When the bookseller Osborne was "impertinent" to him, Johnson knocked him down. Attacked by four ruffians in the street, he held his own until rescued by the watch. When a rude fellow preempted his chair between the side scenes at the theater and refused to yield it, Johnson picked up man and chair and threw them both into the pit. Some of his actions, as when he deliberately swims into a pool he has been told is particularly dangerous, or loads a pistol with a half-dozen balls and fires it off after he has been warned that it will explode, look like foolish bravado. Yet the demonstration of temerity that he is making in such cases is really less personal than racial: he is asserting a principle that it is not good for men to be timorous. Johnson knew the difference between rational courage and callow bravado. His tutor at Oxford asked why he had missed four days' lectures in a row, and young Johnson answered nonchalantly that he had been sliding in Christ Church meadow. Many years later he told that story to Boswell, who congratulated him: "That, Sir, was great fortitude of mind." Johnson corrected him sharply: "No, Sir; stark insensibility." Again he was speaking to a principle: it is unbecoming in the young to slang their qualified elders.

Quieter, slower modes of his courage matter more in the long run. One recalls the resoluteness with which he stood up to persons in high place. The terms of his contemptuous rejection of Lord Chesterfield's tardy patronage are too familiar to need quotation. James Macpherson's *Ossian* was the toast of the age, but Johnson concluded on scholarly grounds that the work was a fraud, and said so loudly and repeatedly. When Macpherson threatened retaliation, presumably by hired bullies, Johnson defied him as follows:

> I received your foolish and impudent letter. Any violence offered me I shall do my best to repel; and what I cannot do for myself, the law shall do for me. I hope I shall never be deterred from detecting what I think a cheat, by the menaces of a ruffian.
>
> What would you have me retract? I thought your book an imposture; I think it an imposture still. For this opinion I have given my reasons to the publick, which I here dare you to refute. Your rage I defy. Your abilities, since your Homer, are not so formidable; and what I hear of your morals, inclines me to pay regard not to what you shall say, but to what you shall prove. You may print this if you will.

Perhaps the most impressive example is one of the quietest. Surprised by the king himself while reading alone in the royal library, Johnson does not stammer or turn servile. He stands and talks at ease of life and letters, one civilized man to another. We see why Goldsmith, merely hearing the tale, feels fluttered and envious.

There was courage in Johnson's cheerful endurance of his marriage to a "flaring and ridiculous" woman old enough to be his mother. His friends thought the match absurd, but Johnson saw nothing odd in it. He loved his Tetty, mourned her heartbrokenly, kept the anniversaries of her death in fasting and prayer, and accepted the care of her blind friend Anna Williams as a lifelong charge. Miss Williams, Miss Carmichael, and Miss Demoulins formed his widower's seraglio, and to them was added the quack doctor Robert Levett. Their only claim upon Johnson was their neediness. He described the domestic scene in a letter to Mrs.

Thrale: "Williams hates every body; Levett hates Demoulins, and does not love Williams; Demoulins hates them both; Poll [Miss Carmichael] loves none of them." Johnson maintained that uneasy company until he or they died.

Few people can have borne poverty with more fortitude or better style. Consider the extraordinary compacting of needy genius when Samuel Johnson and David Garrick, provincial schoolmaster and pupil, both penniless, descend upon the metropolis together one day in 1737: a great subject for an ode that is still unwritten. Because they have no money for a bed, young Johnson and the scapegrace poet Richard Savage walk the night streets of London; undaunted, they attack the ministry in an ebullition of patriotic fervor, and resolve together to "stand by their country." One recalls Johnson's letter to the publisher Edward Cave signed "Yours, *impransus*"—that is, dinnerless. Shortly we see Johnson supping off a plate behind a screen in Cave's shop, ashamed to show his disreputable clothes, and exhilarated to overhear his *Life of Savage* highly praised by a customer, Mr. Harte. The next twenty-five years show Johnson rising slowly, by stubborn application to the higher hackwork, through stages of shabby gentility. He is in his middle fifties before the crown pension of three hundred pounds at last frees him to fold his legs and have out his talk.

With the same sturdy spirit, Johnson endured ill health: his scrofula, his half-blindness, his cough, his asthma, his convulsive tics and totters, his chronic sleeplessness, all joining to create a disposition to indolence that was easy to forgive, but that Johnson scorned in himself with great bitterness. He resisted his indolence in the manliest possible way: by forcing himself to hard and concentrated if spasmodic work. "Sometime in March," he wrote in a late meditation, "I finished the Lives of the Poets, which I wrote in my usual way, dilatorily and hastily, unwilling to work, and working with vigour and haste." His great English *Dictionary* is a more dramatic example. Boswell remarks that the most indolent man in England had performed the most onerous task. When Johnson's Oxford friend Dr. Adams reminds him that he is undertaking to do in three years what the French Academy of forty members needed forty years to complete, Johnson works out a quick equation: "Sir, thus it is. This is the proportion. Let me see; forty times forty is sixteen hundred. As three to sixteen hundred, so is the proportion of an Englishman to a Frenchman." *An* Englishman, mind you.

If we look, on the other hand, at the gloomy grandeur of mood in which Johnson finished that task, after seven years not three, we are brought close to the heart of the larger question: why his life as a whole is so imposing and daunting as a human example. Here is a part of the close of his great preface:

> It may gratify curiosity to inform it, that the *English Dictionary* was written with little assistance of the learned, and without any patronage of the great; not in the soft obscurities of retirement, or under the shelter of academick bowers, but amidst inconvenience and distraction, in sickness and in sorrow: and it may repress the triumph of malignant criticism to observe, that if our language is not here fully displayed, I have only failed in an attempt which no human powers have hitherto completed. . . . I may surely be contented without the praise of perfection, which, if I could obtain, in this gloom of solitude, what would it avail me? I have protracted my work till most of those whom I wished to please, have sunk into the grave, and success and miscarriage are empty sounds: I therefore dismiss it with frigid tranquility, having little to fear or hope from censure or from praise.

In that voice we hear an indurated sadness, not less heavy for being lofty. It is the voice of an Englishman long gripped by the "English malady": the Black Dog of gloom, pessimism, melancholia, hypochondria. Boswell himself appears to have been a classic manic-depressive personality, undiagnosed. When he got up his own magazine he called it the *Hypochondriack*. He observed the morbid syndrome in his friend with fascinated sympathy. Speaking comprehensively during the tour to the Hebrides (1773), Johnson told him that "a vile melancholy" had "made him mad all his life, at least not sober." Boswell concludes: "All his labours, and all his enjoyments, were but temporary interruptions of its baleful influence."

The most moving intimations of Johnson's melancholy, however, are the private ones, such as the obsessive recurrence of the theme in the closet writings that were ultimately published as *Prayers and Meditations*. On Easter Eve of 1761 Johnson wrote: "Since the communion of last Easter, I have led a life so dissipated and useless, and my terrours and perplexities have so much encreased, that I am under great depression and discouragement. . . . I have resolved . . . till I am afraid to resolve again." Three years later he wrote at three o'clock in the morning: "My indolence, since my last reception at the Sacrament, has sunk into grosser sluggishness, and my dissipation spread into wider negligence. A kind of strange oblivion has overspread me, so that I know not what has become of the last year. . . . This is not the life to which heaven is promised." On his birthday in 1780 (September 18), beginning the seventy-second year of a life of notable accomplishment, Johnson was writing heartbrokenly: "Surely I shall not spend my whole life with my own total disapprobation." He had told Boswell that "the great business of his life . . . was to escape from himself." Boswell understood at once the psychology of Johnson's almost pathetic need for company. He preferred it to be the kind that created an intellectual challenge; but almost any company was better than being left alone in the desert of his own spirit.

We see that there is a difference between being brave and being fearless. Johnson was a brave man beset by deadly fears. Boswell put the general case in a properly heroic figure of his own: "His mind resembled the vast amphitheatre, the Colisaeum at Rome. In the centre stood his judgement, which like a mighty gladiator, combated those apprehensions that, like the wild beasts of the *Arena*, were all around in cells, ready to be let out upon him. After a conflict, he drove them back into their dens; but not killing them, they were still assailing him." Johnson showed his greatness not by fearlessness but by the courage with which he faced his fears. His major fears, perhaps his only fears, were two, sufficiently grand: madness and death. In a subsidiary sort of way he feared old age because he associated it with madness and death. Two texts from his meditations give us a sketch of the general ground: on March 30, 1777: "When I survey my past life, I discover nothing but a barren waste of time, with some disorders of body, and disturbances of the mind very near to madness"; and the sentence we have seen from April 21, 1764: "This is not the life to which heaven is promised."

Like Melville's Ahab, Johnson is weak with excess of strength: it is power that makes him specially vulnerable. In his own talk of madness, there is nothing figurative or approximate; when he says madness, he means madness. It is a nice question whether Johnson's melancholy was a real pathology. In one of his "furious" tropes, Melville put the problem of melancholy, the authentic sadness of things as measured against submission to a morbid hopelessness: "There is a wisdom that is woe; but there is a woe that is madness. And there is a Catskill eagle in some souls that can alike dive down into the blackest gorges, and soar out of them again and become invisible in the sunny spaces. And even if he for ever flies within the gorge, that gorge is in the mountains; so that even in his lowest swoop the mountain eagle is still higher than other birds upon the plain, even though they soar." Johnson's fears did not take Ahab's hysterical forms; he would have called Ahab "enthusiastick." His fears were nonetheless grand and acute; his gorge was in the mountains: the abysses of his spirit took place high up. Boswell saw the central irony, that only a mind so powerfully sane could fear subversion so intensely. The fears, in any case, were real. Johnson believed that he stood always on the brink of madness, and he especially feared old age because it portended not only death but senility, a condition in which his mind might lose its powers to resist the great pertinacious enemy. During an evening at Sir Joshua Reynolds's in April 1778, when Johnson was in his seventieth year, one of the company carelessly remarked that he thought it "happy for an old man that insensibility comes upon him." "No, Sir," said Johnson, "I should never be happy by being less rational." He spoke, according to Boswell, "with a noble elevation and disdain."

Talk was the breath of life to Samuel Johnson, but his familiar friends knew there were three subjects on which it was dangerous to try him. One was what he called "bawdy," on which he simply turned his back fastidiously. Another was America: he despised Americans as vulgar rebels, and he could not think of them without rage and contempt. The third forbidden subject was death, which he thought too solemn and terrible for talk, "too awful," as he put it. He would have liked to put death out of his mind, but he dared not do so, and it was the most constant and solemn subject of his meditation. Equally he could be brought to talk of it, reluctantly. He told Boswell that he "never had a moment in which death was not terrible to him." When Boswell asked him if the fear of death was not a thing natural to man, Johnson responded: "So much so, Sir, that the whole of life is but keeping away the thoughts of it." Boswell sketches the scene that ensued one day when he asked Johnson if it were not possible to prepare the mind in such a way as to meet death without fear:

> He answered in a passion, "No, Sir, let it alone. It matters not how a man dies, but how he lives. The act of dying is not of importance, it lasts so short a time." He added (with an earnest look), "A man knows it must be so, and submits. It will do him no good to whine."
> I attempted to continue the conversation. He was so provoked, that he said, "Give us no more of this"; and was thrown into such a state of agitation, that he expressed himself in a way that alarmed and distressed me; shewed an impatience that I should leave him, and when I was going away, he called to me sternly, "Don't let us meet to-morrow."
> I went home exceedingly uneasy.

Strength again, intensified weakness. As Johnson's fear of madness was the fear of a man notably sane, so his fear of death was the fear of a man notably brave and devout. His doubts are the doubts of a believer. I sometimes feel that Johnson was the last True Believer, the last intelligent man to read the Scriptures with literal faith. The right leading is the meditation in which he staggers back, as it were, from the contemplation of his own history: "This is not the life to which heaven is promised." It dawns on us at last that what Johnson fears is not death but what follows death: the undiscovered country. On Good Friday of 1773 Boswell accompanied Johnson to services at St. Clement Danes, and he recalled the "tremendous earnestness" with which he spoke the lines from the litany: "In the hour of death, and at the day of judgement, Good Lord deliver us." Death was fearful not simply as the end of life but as the doorway of doubt, the vestibule of the Last Assizes. When Johnson said to Mrs. Knowles, "No rational man can die without uneasy apprehension," he spoke as a True Believer, full of doubt. Salvation was a beautiful idea but it was by no means an easy universal promise; it was in the highest degree chancy and contingent. When the Redeemer said that at the last day he would set some on the right hand and some on the left, Johnson simply believed him; and he was very much afraid that he would be set on the left. The scene is prepared for one of the great exchanges in the *Life:* " 'As I cannot be *sure* that I have fulfilled the conditions on which salvation is granted, I am afraid I may be one of those who shall be damned' (looking dismally). DR. ADAMS. 'What do you mean by damned?' JOHNSON. (passionately and loudly) 'Sent to Hell, Sir, and punished everlastingly!' " To a True Believer, damnation is damnation.

For Samuel Johnson the end began in a clear and emphatic way, with a stroke, what our doctors now call a cerebrovascular accident (a phrase that might have pleased him by its resonance), during the night of June 16, 1783. He was in his seventy-fourth year, and he had still a year and a half of active life ahead, though of course he could not know that. He woke in the middle of the night and sat up in bed, as was common in his nights; but this time he felt a sudden giddiness, a "confusion and disturbance" in his head that he thought lasted about half a minute. The stroke was evidently a mild one and not paralytic in a serious way. Johnson's way of responding to it has always seemed to me a stunning demonstration of rational courage, especially as measured against the history of his fears.

As a man who has had a hard fall feels himself over for broken bones, so Johnson takes a quick inventory of the powers that matter to him most. As a thinking man, his first fear is that he may have lost his reason. "I was alarmed," he wrote Mrs. Thrale three days later, "and prayed God, that however he might afflict my body, he might spare my understanding." Nothing extraordinary in that—except that Johnson, "to try the integrity of my faculties," composed the prayer, mentally, in Latin verse. The verses were rather poor, he thought; but on the other hand his head was clear enough to recognize that they were poor. So far, so good. Next, being a talking man, he tries his voice. When he finds he cannot speak, he understands that he has suffered a paralytic stroke. He is surprised to feel no pain, and so little apprehension that he wonders whether he has frightened himself unnecessarily all these years about this business of dying. He attacks his muteness in a peremptory way. Reasoning that wine promotes eloquence, he takes a dram, then another. No result. Then, evidently hoping to shake the impacted organs free, he "put [himself] into violent motion." Nothing. He tries again. Nothing. So he goes back to bed and to his later surprise falls peacefully asleep.

Finding himself still speechless at daybreak, he knows he must resort to writing. "My hand, I knew not how or why, made wrong letters," Johnson told Mrs. Thrale; but there was nothing dubious about the sense of the notes he wrote to collect assistance. To his practical friend Edmund Allen he wrote: "It has pleased God, this morning, to deprive me of the powers of speech; and as I do not know but that it may be his further good pleasure to deprive me soon of my senses, I request you will on the receipt of this note, come to me, and act for me, as the exigencies of my case may require." To his old schoolmate the wealthy clergyman Dr. John Taylor, Johnson wrote asking him to come and to bring his medical man, Dr. Heberden. His case, he trusted, was "not past remedy." For Dr. Heberden he summarized his recent ailments, his asthma and his cough and his swollen legs, and the treatment he had received such as opiates and frequent bleedings. Still prescribing for his balky vocal engine, he suggested: "I question if a vomit, vigorous and rough, would not rouse the organs of speech to action."

Within three days, in fact, Johnson had recovered enough voice to pronounce the Lord's Prayer "with no very imperfect articulation." His choice of text for the test was characteristic. By the time he wrote to Boswell on the third of July his doctors considered him essentially cured. But a bell had sounded, and Johnson had heard it. In a note to his dear stepdaughter Lucy Porter, his tone was tender, melancholy, reverent, resolute: "Let us, my dear, pray for one another, and consider our sufferings as notices mercifully given to prepare ourselves for another state. . . . The world passes away, and we are passing with it; but there is, doubtless, another world, which will endure for ever. Let us all fit ourselves for it." Johnson had to face, and he did face, the fact that henceforward he was more or less systematically dying. He went about dying as he had gone about living, with imperfect serenity and with courage, good sense, and the good taste that was so remarkable in a man that many thought of as Ursa Major.

In this penultimate interval his fear of death did not diminish. "O! my friend," he wrote to Dr. Taylor in the spring of his last year, "the approach of death is very dreadful." During a visit to Dr. Adams at Oxford in the summer of 1784, Boswell was present at one of the most moving of the late scenes. At breakfast time the conversation turns upon forms of prayer, and Johnson mentions that he had sometimes thought of composing a treatise on prayer to accompany a selection of prayers by himself and others. His companions urge him warmly to take up the task in earnest, and Johnson is distressed by their importuning: "Do not talk thus of what is so awful. I do not know what time God will allow me in this world." When the others still persist, Johnson moans: "Let me alone, let me alone; I am overpowered." And then, says Boswell, "he put his hands before his face, and reclined for some time upon the table." It is perfectly clear that he is thinking less of prayer than of death, or prayer as a sacramental mode with death as its ultimate object. Johnson now saw himself as inhabiting his final probation. "I hope God will yet grant me a little longer life," he had written Boswell in the preceding autumn, "and make me less unfit to appear before him." Like his biblical namesake he had begun to hear the Almighty calling, "Samuel!"; and he wanted to be ready to answer, "Here am I."

Perhaps we need to understand Johnson's actual physical condition as literally as possible. He put the matter into too small a nutshell in a letter to William Gerard Hamilton about two months before his death: "My diseases are an asthma and a dropsy, and, what is less curable, seventy-five." My layman's guess, rendered more dubious by space and time, is that he had suffered for years from a weak heart, and that his chronic cough and his asthma, like his new dropsy, were related to the poor circulation that was now turning acute in old age. Johnson's habit of life had always been irregular, though it could never have been called dissolute. He could be abstemious, but he found it hard to be moderate. He might fast altogether for a day or two, but ordinarily when there was good food before him he ate voraciously. Apparently he drank no spirits and little wine, but tea he fairly swilled. He was usually overweight and he was certainly too sedentary: he would rather fold his legs than stretch them. Because he was so gloomy and so fond of the company and the talk that relieved his sadness, and because he wished to postpone the long night's trials of body and spirit, he usually sat very late. His cough and what he called the "oppressiveness" in his chest forced him to sleep half-sitting. To relieve his symptoms he took opium derivatives, laudanum and syrup of poppies; but he evidently escaped addiction: he could vary his dose at will or leave it off entirely. The troubled pattern of his nights left him heavy and reluctant in the morning, with the long round to face again. The astonishing thing, of course, is how much work got done in what was after all a chronic condition. Johnson's constitution was rickety but obviously stubborn and tough, and capable of immense spasmodic energy.

But full old age was something new: seventy-five was indeed the incurable ailment. The dropsy that attended the faltering of the heart was the deadly new sign. Johnson now suffered from a general watery swelling accompanied at times by actual edematous tumors from his feet all the way up his legs and into his abdomen. He seems to have imagined the edema as a kind of tide that wished to creep up and drown his vital organs. "A dropsy gains ground upon me," he wrote at one time; and again: "The water breaks its boundaries in some degree." Everything to do with Johnson tended to assume heroic proportions. In February of 1784 he was relieved of twenty pints of fluid. I make that to be ten quarts or two and a half gallons. But he soon "filled again," as he put it, and continued more of less dropsical to the end. Two other new complaints, relatively minor in themselves, elicited typical Johnsonian responses. One was a sarcocele, a fatty cyst or tumor on one of his testicles, of which he wrote to Bennett Langton in September 1783: "I carry about a very troublesome and dangerous complaint, which admits no cure but by the chirurgical knife." He was threatened with amputation (a word, like *cuckoo*, unpleasing to a married ear, at least to a masculine one), but he bore the prospect stoically. Another new problem was gout, which he described to Dr. Mudge as "fierce and fiery," but which the doctor persuaded him almost to welcome as "an antagonist to the palsy."

The minor ailments passed, but the major ones remained, and so did seventy-five. His friends could see that Johnson was slowly failing in body even as his spirit remained undaunted. He showed at times a pathetic wish for reassurance, as when he comforted himself by recollecting that the asthmatic Sir John Floyer has "panted on to ninety," or when William Seward told him that he "saw health returning to his cheek" and Johnson wrung his hand gratefully: "Sir, you are one of the kindest friends I ever had." Still he complained remarkably little. "My nights are restless, and my days, therefore, are heavy," he wrote Lucy Porter in November 1783. "I try, however, to hold up my head as high as I can." This was the norm of the case. A year later, only a month before his death, Johnson was saying: "I will be conquered; I will not capitulate."

Our question is how did Samuel Johnson behave in general after he had received the divine warning. The answer must be that he remained himself, in some ways intensified. He did little formal work; in fact he produced little writing of consequence in his last four years after completing his casual, impressionistic, often brilliant *Lives of the Poets* in 1780. Otherwise Johnson stayed Johnson, perhaps more busily idle than ever. *"But who can run the race with death?"* His question appears, solemnly italicized, in a letter to the musicologist Dr. Burney of August 2, 1784. Yet his strategy was rather like that of Tristram Shandy, who pictured himself as clattering about Europe with death snapping at his heels. Within a couple of weeks of his stroke he was writing to Lucy Porter: "I am going next week into Kent, and purpose to change the air frequently this summer." In fact he went on to change his air more often than ever before, and his movements about England during his final travels were so many that it would be tedious to list them.

Johnson's hectic journeying was obviously a symptom within an old syndrome: his need for company and distraction to hold off the dread of loneliness and torpor that expressed in turn the ultimate fear. "Sickness and solitude press upon me very heavily," he wrote Boswell. "I could bear sickness better, if I were relieved from solitude." For ten years and more Johnson's familiar friends had been dropping around him, and the procession terrified him by its remorselessness. Oliver Goldsmith had gone in 1774 and David Garrick in 1779. Topham Beauclerk died in 1780, and a year later Johnson "felt almost the last flutter" of the pulse of Henry Thrale and "looked for the last time upon the face that for fifteen years had never been turned upon me but with respect and benignity." Even his seraglio was melting away. The death of Robert Levett in 1782 elicited the most grandly simple of Johnson's poems, one in which he took a more benign view of death than he could apply to his own case:

> Then with no throbbing fiery pain,
>   No cold gradation of decay,
> Death broke at once the vital chain,
>   And free'd his soul the nearest way.

A year later passed blind Anna Williams. One begins to wonder if the cat Hodge is still on the scene. In his loneliness Johnson reached out almost feverishly for his surviving friends, visiting and begging visits. He not only attended his club regularly, but collected the surviving members of his old Ivy-lane club and persuaded them to dine with him several times, and he formed a new club to meet three times each week at the Essex Head.

I suppose the main reassurance one takes from Johnson's late sociableness is the evidence that he sustained to the end his established social manner, his bearishness, and his occasional astonishing elegance, and sustained as well his powers of mind and of language, at once massive and sharp. When the great actress Mrs. Siddons paid him a call in the fall of 1783, Johnson noticed that there was no chair ready for her. "Madam," he said, "you who so often occasion a want of seats to other people will the more readily excuse the want of one yourself." They discussed the women in Shakespeare's plays, and Mrs. Siddons said that she thought Queen Katharine in *Henry VIII* the most natural of them all. Johnson agreed with her: "I think so, too, Madam; and whenever you perform it I will once more hobble out to the theatre myself." When the young poetess Helen Maria Williams was presented to him Johnson took her by the hand and recited the finest stanza of her "Ode on the Peace." When she asked after his health on another occasion, Johnson answered: "I am very ill indeed, Madam. I am very ill even when you are near me; what should I be were you at a distance?" When Miss Adams at Oxford remarked that the little pot in which she had made his coffee was the only thing she could call her own, Johnson protested: "I hope you don't reckon my heart as nothing." Writing to his seven-year-old godchild Jane Langton in the summer before his death and admonishing her among other things to "mind your pen, your book, and your needle," he took care to write in large plain characters like printing, to make sure that the little girl could read his letter herself. When a discussion between himself and Richard Burke, son of the great Edmund, had grown heated and then subsided into a sullen silence, uncomfortable for all present, Johnson abruptly said: "Give me your hand, Sir. You were too tedious, and I was too short." Burke assured him: "Sir, I am honoured by your attention in any way." Johnson protested: "Come, Sir, let's have no more of it. We offended one another by our contention; let us not offend the company by our compliments." But really there is no end to it all, until the great end.

It is perfectly clear that Johnson was to be spared the calamity that he called imbecility, and we can document the continuing power of his mind with a few quick incidents. At Oxford, Boswell wagers that Johnson cannot improve his *Rambler* essays, but makes the condition that he must not add to them. Johnson protests at once: "Nay, Sir, there are three ways of making them better;—putting out,—adding,—or correcting." Boswell praises one of Henry Grattan's fervent speeches on behalf of Irish liberty: "We will persevere till there is not one link of the English chain to clank upon the rags of the meanest beggar in Ireland"; Johnson objects swiftly: "Nay, Sir, don't you perceive that one link cannot clank?" After listening to the flow of Johnson's conversation in the coach on the way to Oxford, the American Mrs. Beresford marvels in an aside to Boswell: "How he does talk! Every sentence is an essay." At their inn that evening she is differently impressed to hear the philosopher complain of some poor roast mutton to the waiter: "It is as bad as bad can be: it is ill-fed, ill-killed, ill-kept, and ill-drest."

Johnson would not capitulate, but the time was coming when he must submit to conquest. The shades were visibly drawing in. Boswell sees him for the last time at the end of June 1784. After a chatty evening at Sir Joshua Reynolds's house, Boswell takes him home to Bolt-court in Reynolds's coach:

> He asked me whether I would not go with him to his house; I declined it, from an apprehension that my spirits might sink. We bade adieu to each other affectionately in the carriage. When he had got down upon the foot-pavement, he called out, "Fare you well"; and without looking back, sprung away with a kind of pathetick briskness . . . which seemed to indicate a struggle to conceal uneasiness, and impressed me with a foreboding of our long, long separation.

Boswell must return to Scotland. Of Johnson's remaining actions that we can know, many carry an elegiac air. It occurs to him on July 12, a bit late, surely, to order a stone for the grave of Tetty. He still manages a few provincial junkets, including one to his native Lichfield in which he makes a new friend of a young clergyman, to whom he tells the story of his penitential observance of his boyhood refusal to go with his father to Uttoxeter-market: "A few years ago, I desired to atone for this fault; I went to Uttoxeter in very bad weather, and stood for a considerable time bareheaded in the rain, on the spot where my father's stall used to stand. In contrition I stood, and I hope the penance was expiatory."

From his round of visits Johnson returns to London on November 16, less than a month before his death. Both the asthma and the dropsy, according to Boswell, had now become "more violent and distressful." On the sixth of July he had begun a Latin journal of his illnesses under the title *Aegri Ephemeris* ("A Sick Man's Journal"), but he gave it up on the eighth of November, finding it too tedious and dispiriting. On December 2 Johnson ordered a stone for the graves of his parents and his brother, applying a phrase that could stand as an epitaph for himself: "Let the stone be deep, massy, and hard." At some point in his last days he burned masses of private papers, including, to Boswell's dismay, "two quarto volumes, containing a full, fair, and most particular account of his own life, from his earliest recollection." Johnson's London friends collect about him, sometimes a half-dozen at once in the room. "I am afraid, Sir," says Edmund Burke during his last visit, "such a number of us may be oppressive to you." "No, Sir," Johnson assures him, "it is not so; and I must be in a wretched state, indeed, when your company would not be a delight to me." Burke's reply is tremulous: "My dear Sir, you have always been too good to me."

One could go on indefinitely with the anecdotes, but we can let one stand for the general class. When Dr. Warren hoped that he was better, Johnson answered: "No, Sir; you cannot conceive with what acceleration I advance towards death." He makes his will, leaving most of his tiny estate to form an annuity for his faithful black servant Francis Barber. When Dr. Brockelsby, in answer to Johnson's direct question, tells him that he cannot recover without a miracle, he replies at once: "Then I will take no more physic, not even my opiates; for I have prayed that I may render up my soul to God unclouded." In this resolution he persisted. Of course. The holy sacrament is brought to him at home. On Monday, December 13, young Miss Morris comes to beg his blessing. Johnson turns himself in bed and says, "God bless you, my dear." He did not speak again, and he died that evening without stress or struggle. His old school friend Dr. Taylor read the service in Westminster Abbey, and later William Gerard Hamilton, speaking with what Boswell calls "abrupt felicity," pronounced his noble eulogy: "He has made a chasm, which not only nothing can fill up, but which nothing has a tendency to fill up. Johnson is dead. Let us go to the next best:—there is nobody; no man can be said to put you in mind of Johnson." That seems the right place to stop. I cannot see that we have yet found his equal.

Keats and the Heart's Hornbook

I

We know very well, generally speaking, why we keep reading Keats, and keep trying to find words for his touching and imposing impression upon us: his life and his work form one of the rare configurations that can define the nature of art for us. As King Lear says, in the play Keats loved best of all, "Thou art the thing itself." One is driven to one's private rereadings of the odes and the letters of Keats by their beauty, their wisdom, their difficulty, their young inconclusiveness. But these works are so familiar and beloved to students of poetry, and commentary upon them has grown so huge and expert, that one needs a good excuse for essaying yet another public rereading. Keats's love for Shakespeare is one of many hints suggesting that one profitable context for a new study is the context of the tragic.[1]

By "the tragic" I do not mean here literary, dramatic tragedy, "systematic" tragedy, the codified critical-historical fact and ideal, but something looser and more vulgar and intuitive, "the tragic sense of life," the tragedy that is "common knowledge," the ordinary thinking man's daily awareness of mutability and disaster, the discrepancy between the ideal and the real, between what life promises and what it gives: what A. C. Bradley had in mind when he acknowledged the truth, though the extraliterary truth, of the formula, "Every deathbed is the fifth act of a tragedy." This extraliterary or subliterary or preliterary recognition of generic tragedy has of course a great deal to do with literary tragedy when that is serious and true, for it provides tragedy's grounding in experience, its blood-knowledge of the cosmic rhythm of failure and fatality.

What I propose to argue is that as Keats began to reach that tentative, yet extraordinarily impressive, height of maturity that was allowed him by the awful untimeliness of his death, the conviction that dominated his thought and his art was the radical definition of life as an affair of tragedy, and the determination to make, through art, a strict and warlike

---

1. See also Lionel Trilling's splendid essay, "The Poet as Hero: Keats in His Letters," in *The Opposing Self* (New York: Viking, 1955).

peace with life as so defined. If it is true that Keats became, in this sense, a tragic poet before he died, then it is clear that no poet ever went a longer progress in so short a time. The "little hill" upon which he posed tremulously on "tip-toe" in the first line of the first poem in his first book was a mound of standard romantic attitudes heaped from shards of Spenser, Leigh Hunt, and a little Wordsworth. From that spongy foothold he launched out into the floating faery landscape of *Endymion,* and there he soared passionate and lost: but the next promontory he touched was high and firm, the abstract heroic country of *Hyperion* and the great odes. There "Mister John Keats five feet high" (his own description) stands monumentally. The marvelous boy had also become a tragic poet.

The case should be rested on the greatest of the odes of 1819, for those are the finest, fullest, most "finished" pieces of his work, the truest indication of the kind of thing he was now prepared and determined to write. Writing to George and Georgiana Keats in April 1819, Keats described the "Ode to Psyche," just written, as the "first and only" poem with which he had taken "even moderate pains" (2:105).[2] He goes on: "I think it reads the more richly for it and will I hope encourage me to write other thing[s] in even a more peaceable and healthy spirit" (2:106). The greater odes of the next few months profited by such a temper, and the internal care and the mastery they show warrant our calling them as conclusive, philosophically and artistically, as anything in Keats can be. Ultimately, their spirit is astonishingly "peaceable and healthy," the anagnorisis of the mature tragic spirit, the record of that truce with the nature of experience which I have called strict and warlike.

Surely the best evidence we have of the "prose content" of Keats's mind as he contemplated and composed the odes, and of the order of experience of which they were an emanation, is the long journal-letter he assembled for the American Keatses between the fourteenth of February and the third of May in 1819. In Professor Rollins's edition of the letters this one fills fifty pages. In its sweep of thought, its modulation of tone and spirit, and its depth and variety of insight, the letter is one of the very richest in Keats—which is to say it is one of the richest in our language. We may try to mine it for what it tells us of the "tragic" environment of the odes.

2. All references to Keats's letters are from Hyder Edward Rollins, ed., *The Letters of John Keats, 1814–1821,* 2 vols. (Cambridge: Harvard University Press, copyright 1958) and are reprinted by permission of the publisher and of the President and Fellows of Harvard College. I have preserved Keats's idiosyncrasies of spelling and punctuation except where it was typographically too cumbersome to do so.

When the letter opens, on February 14, it is two months and a half since Keats's brother Tom died of tuberculosis; at least the first sharp shock is past of the experience, in which Keats served as both nurse and mourner, and which he never really successfully assimilated. He and Fanny Brawne have now an "understanding" if not an actual engagement. If Robert Gittings is right, a fling of some sort with Isabella Jones, perhaps a fully consummated affair, is a part of recent memory. His stubborn "sore throat" is beginning to sound ominously chronic. He has recently returned from a dullish, not unpleasant, quietly productive visit to the families of Dilke and Snooks, and one of the letter's first references is to the productive side of it; in a characteristically laconic way he names one of his great poems: "I took down some of the thin paper and wrote on it a little poem call'd 'St. Agnes Eve'" (2:58). Perhaps because he is embarrassed to confess himself deeply involved in a love affair so soon after the death of Tom, Keats gives Fanny only a very casual citation: "Miss Brawne and I have every now and then a chat and a tiff" (2:59). He reports difficulty with *Hyperion:* "I have not gone on with Hyperion—for to tell the truth I have not been in great cue for writing lately—I must wait for the sp[r]ing to rouse me up a little" (2:62). (Before the letter is finished we are to see that the spring had roused him up to the great odes.) He performs one of his antiparsonic "rhodomontades." He gives a feeling salute to the pleasures of claret, light and bright in tone, yet in language and intensity that are to lead straight into the serious imagery of two of the odes, those to Melancholy and the Nightingale:

> now I like Claret whenever I can Have Claret I must drink it.—'t is the only palate affair that I am at all sensual in. . . . if you could make some wine like Claret to d[r]ink on summer evenings in an arbour! For really 't is so fine—it fills . . . one's mouth with a gushing freshness—then goes down cool and feverless—then you do not feel it quarreling with your liver—no it is rather a Peace maker and lies as quiet as it did in the grape. (2:64)

In the same "sensual" train, recollection of his other "palate passion," game—"I must plead guilty to the breast of a Partridge, the back of a hare, the backbone of a grouse, the wing and side of a Pheasant and a Woodcock passim" (2:64–65)—reminds him that "the Lady whom I met at Hastings" (probably Isabella Jones) has been plying him so heavily with presents of game that he has been able to give much of it away.

Thus far all has been pleasant gossip and chitchat, nothing to prepare us for the deeps to come; then they begin to arrive. Here are the last words for February 19: "A Man's life of any worth is a continual allegory—and very few eyes can see the Mystery of his life—a life like the scriptures, figurative. . . . Lord Byron cuts a figure—but he is not figurative—Shakespeare led a life of Allegory; his works are the comments on it" (2:67). The passage makes several important suggestions about Keats's thinking and about the right way to read his verse. We have been repeatedly warned, new-critically, to read the poems in freestanding isolation, as naked artifacts, things-in-themselves, not to corrupt them by adducing irrelevant prose-informations. Keats's odes sustain that kind of clinical reading with nearly perfect aplomb. But this passage shows, surely, that Keats himself thought of poetry as a direct apprehension of significant experience, an entrapment in language of the "allegory" in life, its moments of fullest "figurative" gesture. Keats knew no more about the life of Shakespeare than we do; he knew a great deal of more or less accurate gossip about the life of Byron. He assumes that one is a great life, in the sense of being allegorical, figurative, and the other not great because it is not so, on the evidence of what he knows of the literature, not of the life. His assumption is gratuitous, intuitive. He speaks of what he thinks "must" be true, what he wishes to be true. Thus what he announces here is a personal ideal of literature and life and of their relation: the greatest works, the scriptural kind, are comments upon a significant, because "allegorical," life. We would do well, in reading the work of a writer who believes in this way, to make any appropriate use we can of the surrounding prose-informations.

For our context of tragedy the passage has other important information. Keats nominates as the archetype of the allegorical life, and hence as the object of highest admiration, the giant of modern tragedy, Shakespeare, whom he elsewhere wistfully summoned to be his "presidor." The view he takes of the relation between literature and personality is immensely suggestive, too. For he is not saying that literature is hotly subjective, a direct offering of the self in language, an unmodulated *cri du coeur*. It was Keats, after all, who applied to Wordsworth the devastating phrase "the egotistical sublime." What he asks for here, clearly, is not the exploitation of personality, but the sublimation of self into symbol, the recognition of the representative in an individual's experience: the key words are "allegory," "scriptures," "figurative." This kind of nearly classical detachment is one of the habits of mind that make one question the textbook designation of Keats as "Romantic" poet. Repeatedly in the letters, Keats speaks of "disinterestedness" as an ethical ideal, the right way for a good man to behave. In art he proposes a corollary ideal of "unobtrusiveness":

We hate poetry that has a palpable design upon us—and if we do not agree, seems to put its hand in its breeches pocket. Poetry should be great and unobtrusive, a thing which enters into one's soul, and does not startle it or amaze it with itself but with its subject.—How beautiful are the retired flowers! how would they lose their beauty were they to throng into the highway crying out, "admire me I am a violet! dote upon me I am a primrose!" Modern poets differ from the Elizabethans in this. . . . Why should we be of the tribe of Manasseh, when we can wander with Esau? (1:224)

The ideal is of course specifically classical. It also seems to me specifically tragic, expressing the quality of largeness, of representativeness, of "disinterestedness," that we associate with the grandest literary tragedies, and with the tragic sense of life when that is complete and articulate.

The nineteenth of March finds Keats apparently confirmed in a mood of pleasant lassitude, "a sort of temper indolent and supremely careless." "In this state of effeminacy," he says,

> the fibres of the brain are relaxed in common with the rest of the body, and to such a happy degree that pleasure has no show of enticement and pain no unbearable frown. Neither Poetry, nor Ambition, nor Love have any alertness of countenance as they pass by me: they seem rather like three figures on a greek vase—a Man and two women—whom no one but myself could distinguish in their disguisement. (2:78-79)

The image makes a clear presentiment of the "Ode on Indolence"; less clearly, it anticipates the "Ode on a Grecian Urn," and it may even point toward the gleaner of "To Autumn." Keats's dominant mood in this whole period is in fact as much autumnal as springlike, though one feels that he hardly knows it. Keats's poetical career is so terribly short that we almost feel that we can hold it all in a single view, and what one feels about this spring and summer of 1819 is that they form a watershed, an unsuspectedly fertile plateau, of his creative life. In this splendid garnering autumn of his youth, before that chronic "sore throat" had manifested its full fatality, he was resting and thinking and reading, savoring life and love, scorning all his work to date, and writing the best of his poems—all without knowing that his temper was anything more than "languor" and "laziness," as he called it. Had he any suspicion how short was his lease? One would like to know. I cannot avoid the feeling that a half-conscious anticipation of the end of things thickens and enriches the poems and the letters of these months.

His indolent mood is interrupted by a bit of *lacrimae rerum*, a note from Haslam portending the death of his father. This sets under way a complicated and interesting train of thought. Keats is moved first to draw up the formula of the treacherousness and mutability of life:

> This is the world—thus we cannot expect to give way many hours to pleasure—Circumstances are like Clouds continually gathering and bursting—While we are laughing the seed of some trouble is put into . . . the wide arable land of events—while we are laughing it sprouts [i]t grows and suddenly bears a poison fruit which we must pluck. (2:79)

Then his recognition that his involvement in Haslam's grief is shallow as compared to the way he feels his own troubles makes him recall a major theme, his ideal of "disinterested" humanity:

> Even so we have leisure to reason on the misfortune of our friends; our own touch us too nearly for words. Very few men have ever arrived at a complete disinterestedness of Mind; very few have been influenced by a pure desire of the benefit of others—in the greater part of the Benefactors [of] . . . Humanity some meretricious motive has sullied their greatness—some melodramatic scenery has fascinated them—From the manner in which I feel Haslam's misfortune I perceive how far I am from any humble standard of disinterestedness. (2:79)

From the idealism of this he reverts to what seems a candid acceptance of the predatory balance of the order of nature:

> For in wild nature the Hawk would loose his Breakfast of Robins and the Robin his of Worms The Lion must starve as well as the Swallow—The greater part of Men make their way with the same instinctiveness, the same unwandering eye from their purposes, the same animal eagerness as the Hawk—The Hawk wants a Mate, so does the Man—look at them both they set about it and procure on[e] in the same manner—They want both a nest and they both set about one in the same manner. (2:79)

Keats is adopting, for the moment, uncomfortably, the posture of scientific "objectivity," "facing facts": "This is what makes the Amusement of Life—to a speculative Mind" (2:79-80). But this is a false posture for Keats, and he cannot hold it. The poetic epistle to Reynolds of a year earlier records his true native horror at the spectacle of nature seen "too deep into the sea." He is not permanently interested in the predatory norm, but in the heroic exceptions, the men who rise to selflessness:

> But then as Wordsworth says, "we have all one human heart"—there is an ellectric fire in human nature tending to purify—so that among these human creature[s] there is continually some birth of new heroism—The pity is that we must wonder at it: as we should at finding a pearl in rubbish—I have no doubt that thousands of people never heard of have had hearts comp[l]etely

disinterested: I can remember but two—Socrates and Jesus—their Histories evince it. (2:80)

Keats is trying to settle for himself, in this long portion of the long letter, a workable relation between ideality and reality, and, as several passages show, he is also trying to synthesize some heavy doses of Hazlitt's pragmatism without a sublimation unacceptable to the honesty of his own mind. The whole course of his thought here is twisting and insecure and touchingly diffident; he makes his own necessary confession of amateurishness:

> Even here though I myself am pursuing the same instinctive course as the veriest human animal you can think of—I am however young writing at random—straining at particles of light in the midst of a great darkness—without knowing the bearing of any one assertion of any opinion. Yet may I not in this be free from sin? . . . Give me this credit—Do you not think I strive—to know myself? (2:80-81)

Ultimately he closes this argument by shifting his direction once more; he brings back his old insistence that abstract conviction must be first "proved upon our pulses," must move through the senses and the passions: "Nothing ever becomes real till it is experienced—Even a proverb is no proverb to you till your Life has illustrated it" (2:81). The letter rises higher later, to more secure morality and aesthetics; here what moves one is the young largeness of the mind and heart, a part of that quality Lionel Trilling, following Shaw, justly called the "geniality" of Keats.

Now he begins to feel embarrassed that he has remained so serious so long. With his typical touching magnanimity, Keats tries to lighten the weight of his own speculation for his brother and his sister-in-law by apologizing for the depth of what he has said and what he knows he is about to say:

> I am ever affraid that your anxiety for me will lead you to fear for the violence of my temperament continually smothered down: for that reason I did not intend to have sent you the following sonnet—but look over the two last pages and ask yourselves whether I have not that in me which will well bear the buffets of the world. It will be the best comment on my sonnet; it will show you that it was written with no Agony but that of ignorance; with no thirst of any thing but knowledge when pushed to the point though the first steps to it were throug[h] my human passions—they went away, and I wrote with my Mind—and perhaps I must confess a little bit of my heart. (2:81)

But the disclaimer doesn't really "work." It is too clear from tone and pressure in the prose and in the draft of the sonnet that the impelling "Agony" rises out of "knowledge," or at least conviction, as much as out of "ignorance." Though he deprecates the bitterness of the sonnet, its impelling emotions emerge, shamefaced but stubborn, in the phrase "a little bit of my heart."

I take it that the sonnet itself is an important text in support of my reading of Keats as tragic poet. Its death imagery is a part of the encircling mood of the odes, where the idea of death will be variously qualified and complicated. Line 11 is a study for a central image of the "Ode to a Nightingale": "to cease upon the midnight with no pain."

> Why did I laugh tonight? No voice will tell:
>   No God, no Deamon of severe response
> Deigns to reply from heaven or from Hell.—
>   Then to my human heart I turn at once—
> Heart! thou and I are here sad and alone;
>   Say, wherefore did I laugh? O mortal pain!
> O Darkness! Darkness! ever must I moan
>   To question Heaven and Hell and Heart in vain!
> Why did I laugh? I know this being's lease,
>   My fancy to its utmost blisses spreads:
> Yet could I on this very midnight cease,
>   And the world's gaudy ensigns see in shreds.
> Verse, fame and Beauty are intense indeed
>   But Death intenser—Death is Life's high meed.

The blank death-wishing bitterness of such a poem does not of course define anything like the ultimate tragic vision; it embodies only its primitive grounding in the *lacrimae-rerum* landscape. But it does confess the reality of the landscape. The wonderful sentence that concludes this long entry for March 19 rounds the contradictions of Keats's "speculations" in the one perfect way, and it greatly amplifies the developing tragic vision by suggesting the crucial reconciling paradox—wholeness preserved and bitterness assimilated: "I went to bed, and enjoyed an uninterrupted sleep—Sane I went to bed and sane I arose" (2:82). Tragedy is never fretful, never mad.

The last, particularly grand, long section of the letter begins on April 15 and ends May 3. As usual Keats resumes with the accumulated small news of the interval of silence, and as usual the texture of the letter thickens as he exhausts his gossip and begins to dig into the current workings of his own mind. The indolent fit still grips him; nothing yet tells him that he is resting his fibers for his last great creative surge. He sounds the recurrent fiscal note of the year: "I am still at a stand in versifying—I cannot do it yet with any pleasure—I mean however to look round at my resources and means—and see what I can do without poetry" (2:84). A passage of a dozen or so tantalizing lines records a shorthand version of a conversation, more properly a monologue, with the fabulous elliptical talker Coleridge, covering eighteen headings beginning with "Nightingales" and ending with "Good morning," following a chance meeting and a walk at his "alderman-after dinner pace for near two miles" (2:88). This is succeeded by three burlesque Spenserian stanzas taking off his raffish housemate Brown—all roughly efficient ironic comedy, coming easily to the left hand, costing him little. Then he recounts a recent dream which rose out of his reading in Dante, the central image in which becomes an important figure in the "Ode to Psyche":

> The dream was one of the most delightful enjoyments I ever had in my life—I floated about the whirling atmosphere as it is described with a beautiful figure to whose lips mine were joined as it seem'd for an age—and in the midst of all this cold and darkness I was warm—even flowery tree tops sprung up and we rested on them sometimes with the lightness of a cloud till the wind blew us away again—I tried a Sonnet upon it—There are fourteen lines but nothing of what I felt in it—o that I could dream it every night. (2:91)

He inserts the sonnet itself, the beautiful one beginning, "As Hermes once took to his feathers light," and ending, "Pale were the lips I kiss'd and fair the fo[r]m / I floated with about that melancholy storm"—all intensely pathetic, in its ghostly half-fulfillment, as a metaphor of his star-crossed affair with Fanny. After this he makes one of his characteristic reversals of tone and directs a long passage of gusty comic raillery at Georgiana. Then, again with no warning, and with no preface except "Wednesday Evening," comes one of the capital poems, a draft of "La Belle Dame sans Merci."

We approach now the letter's crown, the famous "vale of Soul-making" passage, a breathless paragraph that fills three and a half printed pages and closes the long entry for April 21. Keats has been reading, he says, "two very different books Robertson's America and Voltaire's Siecle de Louis xiv" (2:100). In reflecting on these books (a total of nine volumes), he has been struck, first, by the contrast between the rude and the sophisticated society; but then, pursuing the idea, he has dredged up a revelation that has horrified him—the fact of their deeper similarity: "In How lamentabl[e] a case do we see the great body of the people in both instances" (2:100–101). What has come to him is the conviction that the difficulty of man's estate results not from the social order but from the genes of species and fate: thus it looks irredeemable. Such, at least, is his first hypothesis, and it takes its text, we should note, from *King Lear*, showing once more how Shakespeare, and especially that play, habitually accompanied Keats in his deepest speculations:

> The whole appears to resolve into this—that Man is originally "a poor forked creature" subject to the same mischances as a beast of the forest, destined to hardships and disquietiude of some kind or other. If he improves by degrees his bodily accommodations and comforts—at each stage, at each accent there are waiting for him a fresh set of annoyances—he is mortal and there is still a heaven with its Stars abov[e] his head. The most interesting question that can come before us is, How far by the persevering endeavours of a seldom appearing Socrates Mankind may be made happy. (2:101)

But candor drives him to say that he finds unacceptably sentimental his whole idealistic concept of human perfectibility (he has spoken patronizingly of Dilke in an earlier journal-letter as a "Godwin perfectibility Man"); the details in which he amplifies his pragmatic disenchantment crudely dramatize the impossibility of earthly well-being:

> But in truth I do not at all believe in this sort of perfectibility—the nature of the world will not admit of it—the inhabitants of the world will correspond to itself—Let the fish philosophise the ice away from the Rivers in winter time and they shall be at continual play in the tepid delight of summer. Look at the Poles and at the sands of Africa, Whirlpools and volcanoes—Let men exterminate them and I will say that they may arrive at earthly Happiness—The point at which Man may arrive is as far as the paralel state in inanimate nature and no further—For instance suppose a rose to have sensation, it blooms on a beautiful morning it enjoys itself—but there comes a cold wind, a hot sun—it cannot escape it, it cannot destroy its annoyances—they are as native to the world as itself: no more can man be happy in spite, the world[l]y elements will prey upon his nature. (2:101)

The passage that follows contains the heart of Keats as man, as thinker, and as tragic poet. It forms a complicated web of rejections and acceptances. He has already rejected the adolescent notion of the world as a place of sentimental felicity. He now rejects the conclusion that would seem to follow, that life on earth is only a drab and hopeless interregnum; he then specifically rejects the Christian corollary of that view, that we are rescued from the interregnum by a deus ex machina immortality. He now posits his great acceptances—of death as the limit of life, of the enmity of fate to the individual, of the duty of man to assemble his joy out of the parts of his being infallibly scattered by the Furies of destiny. The first lines of the passage summarize the whole argument:

> The common cognomen of this world among the misguided and superstitious is "a vale of tears" from which we are to be redeemed by a certain

arbit[r]ary interposition of God and taken to Heaven—What a little circumscribe[d] straightened notion! Call the world if you Please "The vale of Soul-making" Then you will find out the use of the world. (2:101-2)

Keats then labors to clarify his use of "Soul." He equates it, we see, with "identity"; but by identity he means something larger than "personality," or consciousness of self: he means, in fact, almost the opposite—an assembled wholeness, an achieved invulnerability. The "bliss peculiar to each ones individual existence" is the joyous sense of that wholeness; and the proper "use of the world," the world that we know, is that only such a world can provide a discipline rigorous enough to accomplish such wholeness.

> I say "Soul making" Soul as distinguished from an Intelligence—There may be intelligences or sparks of the divinity in millions—but they are not Souls . . . till they acquire identities, till each one is personally itself. . . . How then are these sparks which are God to have identity given them—so as ever to posses a bliss peculiar to each ones individual existence? How, but by the medium of a world like this? This point I sincerely wish to consider because I think it a grander system of salvation than the chrysteain religion—or rather it is a system of Spirit-creation. (2:102)

He then sums up his speculation in a figure of splendid simplicity:

> I will call the world a School instituted for the purpose of teaching little children to read—I will call the human heart the horn book used in that School—and I will call the Child able to read, the Soul made from that school and its hornbook. Do you not see how necessary a World of Pains and troubles is to school an Intelligence and make it a soul? A Place where the heart must feel and suffer in a thousand diverse ways! Not merely is the Heart a Hornbook, It is the Minds Bible, it is the Minds experience, it is the teat from which the Mind or intelligence sucks its identity. . . . This appears to me a faint sketch of a system of Salvation which does not affront our reason and humanity. (2:102-3)

Finally, fearing he still has not made himself clear, Keats goes on to recapitulate his whole argument.

Drafts of poems fill most of the remaining pages of the long letter—two mediocre sonnets on Fame, the beautiful sonnet "To Sleep," which begins, "O soft embalmer of the still midnight," and ends with the dark velvet lines, "Turn the Key deftly in the oiled wards / And seal the hushed Casket of my Soul," the final sonnet an experiment in getting rid of the "pouncing rhymes" of the conventional form, which points toward the great ode stanza now forming in the work of these spring days. Then this magnificent letter ends with a serene image of the season itself, an image which reappears in the "Ode to a Nightingale," and which forms as well a perfect figure for that mood of calm transcendence which makes one of the last movements in the "tragic" sequence: "this is the 3 of May and every thing is in delightful forwardness; the violets are not withered, before the peeping of the first rose" (2:109). We may discover in the lines "To Sleep," in Keats's setting for the "Ode to Psyche," and in the draft of the ode itself that immediately follows, the kind of poetry that was beginning to come out of the deep philosophical equipoise at which he had arrived in the thought of these months.

It is difficult not to claim too much for such an appealing document as this letter, but it is also important to claim enough. This is after all not a finished essay in ethics or aesthetics, and Keats was after all a very young man. But, though he was half-lettered, he was also an extraordinarily brilliant and high-principled young man. And so, though the thought here is often rude or incomplete, or merely derivative (especially from Hazlitt and Locke), it is also strangely mellow, beautifully intelligent, and movingly humane. We have already seen Keats's own exactly proper apology: "I am however young writing at random—straining at particles of light in the midst of a great darkness. . . . Yet may I not in this be free from sin?" I am far from claiming that Keats was putting together here anything like a conscious or coherent "theory of tragedy"; what I do suggest is that this most comprehensive of all the prose expressions of Keats's "sense of life" assembles a definition of experience as a generically tragic order, and that this, the most conclusive view of life he lived to record, formed the subject matter and the impelling emotion of the greatest of his odes. These are the major motives in Keats's tragic sense of life as I see them emerging in the letter: a high-serious "Melancholy," recognizing the world as a place of immanent defeat and death; the invocation of Shakespeare as his "presidor"; the criterion of "disinterestedness," calling for objective selflessness and a clinical use of personal experience as "figurative," as representative and symbolic; his agnostic rejection of other-worldly solutions of tragic fact, and the determination to use the resources of the mind and heart in this world to make a viable peace with fatal reality; the general compelling tendency to reconcile the complex sadness of experience in an oxymoronic tragic joy—"the bitter Sweet of this Shakespearean fruit," as he called it in his sonnet on *King Lear*. Most of these motives are finely compressed in a sentence in a famous letter to Reynolds: "Until we are sick, we understand not;—in fine, as Byron says, 'Knowledge is Sorrow'; and I go on to say that 'Sorrow is Wisdom'—and further for aught we can know for certainty! 'Wisdom is folly' " (1:279).

The awful telescoping of Keats's life forced this kind of insight upon him. The marvelous thing is the balance; never, at least never until the end when his emotional control began to go to pieces with the dissolution of his body, was his passion ever sour or frantic. The serenely disciplined poise of it all, the sweetness, is intensely moving to witness. Writing to Shelley, whose behavior to Keats was beautiful throughout, and who had written to offer a haven in Italy to the young poet dying of the "disease particularly fond of people who write such good verses as you have done," Keats embodied his inner reconciliation, his complicated peace, in one of the finest of his figures: "My imagination is a Monastry and I am its Monk" (2:323). "Extraordina[r]y talk for the writer of Endymion," as he himself notes. But Keats in 1820 was not merely the writer of that "green tangle," as Bridges called it; he was the composer of the ode "To Autumn": he was "pick'd up and sorted to a pip."

II

It is wise to give in at once to the temptation to think of Keats's great odes of 1819 as in essence a single long poem—or at least, as Professor Garrod suggested, as an "ode-sequence." But I insist that one must not detach "To Autumn" from the sequence, as Garrod and most other commentators like to do; though it comes later by a few months, it is in every way a vital part of the total organism. It is certain that Keats did not think of his odes as one poem, and very likely that he did not think of them as an organic sequence. But in our aloofness from the creative act, we are entitled to specify the relatedness in tone and theme that was probably half-conscious for Keats; and so long as we do not destroy the integrity of the odes as separate poems we will profit legitimately from the light that comes from reading them as a composite work of art.

Indeed I should like to impose a still tighter and more arbitrary pattern—because I think the pattern exists in fact and, by marking the major stages in the definition of Keats as tragic poet, reveals a crucial truth. That pattern eliminates the "Ode to Psyche" and the "Ode on Indolence" and is composed of, in order, the "Ode on Melancholy," the "Ode to a Nightingale," the "Ode on a Grecian Urn," and "To Autumn." Yet it is very important to see that the generating mood of all the odes originates, however unpromisingly, in the "Ode on Indolence." Keats's mood of dreamy lassitude, which is described so often in the letters of 1819, and which is met in this poem in "Ripe was the drowsy hour; / The blissful cloud of summer-indolence" and "drowsy noons, / And evenings steep'd in honied indolence," becomes, as it moves from body into mind and from vagary into passion, the entranced yet vivid introspection that precipitates the greater odes. "The true voice" of Keats's marvelously fertile indolence begins to speak in the "Ode on Melancholy," and at last the rather unpleasantly sprawling satisfaction of the poet in the "Ode on Indolence" matures into the erect, impersonal, complexly symbolic figure of the most significant image in Keats: the gleaner of "To Autumn," who "dost keep / Steady thy laden head."

The "Ode on Melancholy" and "To Autumn" form a kind of frame around the picture of Keats as tragic artist, in the sense that the one sets the precipitating negative conviction and the other answers it positively by accepting and then transmuting the negative; within that frame the other two odes labor toward the positive but stop short. In the "Ode on Melancholy" Keats conducts a tragic initiate through *lacrimae rerum* to a refuge that proves bitterly paradoxical: "Ay, in the very temple of Delight / Veil'd Melancholy has her sovran shrine." The definition of sadness is acid and hopeless and takes its perverse satisfaction from a kind of heroic vagueness or grandly magnified helplessness at the end of the poem: "His soul shall taste the sadness of her might, / And be among her cloudy trophies hung." Within the scope of this poem the mood is definitive and perfectly realized; but within the scheme of the "ode-sequence" the mood is inconclusive. The argument is one that had to be cleared away before movement could take place, a brush-burning before the new seeding.

In the "Ode to a Nightingale" Keats continues his waking-dream state of the "Ode on Indolence," but with an important shift of accent and direction. The mood of reverie has matured markedly, grown questing and intense and creative; reverie has become the alembic of the passions and the intellect. And so the real mood of the poem is directed not by Indolence but by Melancholy; like the "Ode on a Grecian Urn" and "To Autumn," the "Ode to a Nightingale" really lives in the climate of tragic despair. Like them, also, it tries to escape from that despair, or to make peace within it. As in "To Autumn," Keats tries to build his vehicle of escape from the furnishings of nature. And if we compare the nature imagery of the "Nightingale" with that of the "Ode to Psyche," where there is little irruption of the personal dilemma, we see how strikingly the temper of Keats's introspection has deepened and warmed in the course of working through the linked moods of the spring odes. The grand resolution he reaches in the autumn ode is here only a haunting and beautiful irresolution. But that very irresolution becomes, I believe, this poem's basic theme and the core of its significance in the formation of the poet's tragic view.

Irresolution affects the poem's texture and its structure. The "Ode on Melancholy" dwelt in an area of sad certainty in its confident analysis of absolute despair; this ode, which feels no certainty, only the rich doubt of passionate, salvatory, perfectionist aspiration, is marked by greater looseness of thought, of organization, and of detail. Keats's position in the poem is now much more intimately subjective, and this means that things are seen in softer outlines and sweeter tones, that they are less firmly and rationally controlled. The dramatic condition of the poem is one of interaction, basically of opposition, between the aspiring and the achieving spirit, poet and bird—between "My heart aches" and "thine Happiness." Two motifs are fundamental: the bird's symbolic embodiment of immutable ideality, especially the superhuman power to transcend time and the vale of tears, and the movement of the dramatic line, which rises to a hesitant, imperfect identification in the fourth and fifth stanzas, then slowly collapses to a quiet confession of defeat. Stanza 7 sums up the symbolic oppositions of the theme. The poet, involved in a brief ironic illusion of permanence on "this passing night," confronts his mutability in confessing the uniqueness of the bird's transcendent power of speech to "emperor and clown," to the exiled Ruth, to the persons of romantic fable; the beauty makes bearable the fatality.

The "Ode on a Grecian Urn" is an intricately manipulated conceit, beautifully observed and reasoned. The voluble artifact, the urn, is invited to speak its abstract music to the abstracted ear—to "Pipe to the spirit ditties of no tone"—and it speaks, through eloquent concrete images and gnomic text, sufficient wisdom. In terms of the tragic vision, the movement of the poem is substantially that of the "Ode to a Nightingale": the questing spirit, still trapped in the vale of Melancholy, mining his passionate bemusement in search of succor and release, turns for salvation to the world of created art. He receives comfort and illumination and finally a great abstract insight, but no full salvation. The "Ode on a Grecian Urn" again confirms human life as an order of merely negative tragedy—or pathos; it again confirms high art as a contrasted order of achieved magnificence. Yet the effect of the famous crux of the closing lines is both to amplify and to undercut the "established" themes, and thereby to force a radical shift in our standard despair.

One thing the eloquent urn proposes in its equation of Beauty and

Truth, it seems to me, is the further dry-eyed insight that Despair is also Truth. It is the position assumed at the end of the "Ode on Melancholy" and, with complications, at the end of the "Ode to a Nightingale." But when we can call the insight into Despairing Truth an insight into Beauty as well, we have begun to mature beyond pathos into tragedy and to move toward that point where we stand not annihilated by Truth but reassembled by it. The "Ode on a Grecian Urn" makes a crucial gesture toward the fulfillment of the tragic sense of life. It shows a man driven out of life into thought, out of thought into art, and out of art back into thought. But Keats's decisive motion here has yet to be welcomed into the self, reembodied, and projected beyond the self in an adequately complex and active form; these are the things that take place in the multifoliate image of the last ode.

I feel that the ode "To Autumn," in its deceptive seeming simplicity, is the least understood and the most undervalued of Keats's poems. Most critics have said, in effect, that it is formally the most perfect, thematically the thinnest of the great odes, a technical masterpiece but thoughtless; it is a beautiful landscape but static, mute, without significance beyond its own frame. Allen Tate puts the type-judgment succinctly, and we can borrow that as a sally-port for a new approach to the poet-philosopher Keats had become: " 'Ode to Autumn' is a very nearly perfect piece of style but it has little to say."

Middleton Murry wrote of the ode as follows:

> It need not be pointed out with a finger how deeply Shakespearean that perfect poem is—Shakespearean in its rich and opulent serenity of mood, Shakespearean in its lovely and large periodic movement, like the drawing of a deep, full breath. . . . It is the perfect and unforced utterance of the truth contained in the magic words: "Ripeness is all."

F. R. Leavis's brusque rebuttal to this passage in Murry reconstitutes the usual reading of the poem:

> Such talk is extravagant, and does not further the appreciation of Keats. No one could have found that order of significance in the Ode merely by inspecting the Ode itself. The ripeness with which Keats is concerned is the physical ripeness of autumn, and his genius manifests itself in the sensuous richness with which he renders this in poetry, without the least touch of artistic overripeness.

The lush looseness of the one and the dry concentration of the other are characteristic of the two critics. And while both are right in a way, Murry, rhapsodizing and all, seems to me righter. I feel that he is not extravagant but newly just when he places the ode in the context of Shakespeare and of tragedy, and that that "order of significance" can be found in the ode itself, in its nature and its stature.

My special sense of "To Autumn" is that it is the ode in which the warring extremes of the tragic sense of life are finally reconciled and liberated. Far from having "little to say," it is crowded with audible wisdom, and the chief thing it says is indeed Edgar's "Ripeness is all"; or, to avoid the elementary confusion with the "ripe" season that troubles Leavis, perhaps Hamlet's "The readiness is all" would serve better. I agree that the ode seems to say little—we do not see its lips move. But poetry can speak in ways other than loud logical discourse. One of these ways of mute eloquence is the speaking drama of imagery.

The first stanza is made up almost entirely of a crowded catalog of sight images that record the immense fruitfulness of the season by multiplying visions of fullness, heaviness, ripeness—a sensation of fruition now absolute and perfect. But one gradually comes to realize that the images are not so much visual as tactual; the objects seen are more importantly felt, and this empathic effect is carried by the strikingly simple, active, vigorous verbs of touch and pressure: "load," "bless," "bend," "fill," "swell," "plump," "set budding," and "o'er-brimmed."

In stanza 2 the personification of Autumn has become intimate and detailed, and the form of the gleaner has become a specific figure of focus. Keats sets that figure in a sequence of stylized offices that are really attitudes or postures more than actions, forming a striking and very subtle combination of understated dramatic moods. The moods are passive—"careless," "steady," "patient"—suspended and fixed while half-complete. The image-sense is again notably empathic, combining sensations of sight, smell, touch, taste; but the stanza's impression is defined almost more significantly by the missing sense, sound: an interesting and complex soundlessness renders, silently, the coordinating mood of dreamy suspension.

The closing stanza is dominated by that sense that was withheld in stanza 2. The resumption here, after the silence, of the droning hum of autumnal noises reminds one of the cry of the autumn locust—that slightly syncopated, slightly off-key song, rising to its crescendo, stopping sharp off, beginning again; the locust appears in person in the "hedge-crickets" of the ninth line. At any rate, almost all the images here are auditory ones; we may therefore be struck first by the shift, since the first stanza, in the sound of the verse, the shift to a kind of thin minor that is carried by the multiplication of short *i* and *e* sounds. Hearing the developed contrast to the confident, robust roundness of sound in stanza 1 offers an elementary insight into the poem; if that leads us to a closer look at the images of the third stanza in order to see by what means other than sound the effect is achieved, we have begun our first real penetration.

For if we really scrutinize those images, we see that they fall into an elaborate pattern of intentional equivocation. Virtually every image or pair of images forms a paradox, an oxymoron: the images make two gestures, promising and threatening; celebrate two moods, joyful and sorrowful; look in two directions, backward to summer, forward to winter, backward to life, forward to death. The opposition that is set under way by the response of "thy music" to the "songs of Spring" is carried out in beautiful and explicit detail in the images that follow. First the "barred clouds" reach all the way back to the opening stanza to qualify softly its "maturing sun" and "warm days." Then, within the frame of the third stanza alone, "bloom" is counterposed to "dying"; "stubble" is opposed to "rosy." In line 5 "wailful" and "mourn" undercut and darkly color our notions of a "choir" as a positive voice of joy or praise or a merely neutral voice of solemnity. In line 6 does Keats choose "sallows" for its color connotations instead of the less evocative "willows"? Clearly, at any rate, "borne aloft" is counterposed to "sinking" as "lives" is to "dies." The lambs now "full-grown" deny their spring; their "bleat" is their standard cry, but our extra sense of it is sad and pathetic. The hedge-crickets are the stanza's only largely neutral image; but even that neutrality is conditioned by their association with the passing season and so with evanescence. The two bird images that complete the poem round out the oxymoronic complex: the song of the redbreast is reduced to a "treble soft"; and the swallows' "twitter" is plaintive, emaciated, anticipatory—portentous, as is their very "gathering."

Significantly, the only other place in which Keats uses this elaborate pattern of paradox is in the "Cave of Quietude" passage in *Endymion*, his first embodiment of tragic reconciliation. We cannot escape its presence here at the end of the ode "To Autumn," and it must drive us back to review the first two stanzas and ask whether the paradox is everywhere in the poem and what force it has in the total meaning. Then we realize at last that the oxymoron was subtly anticipated from the beginning by Keats's piecemeal assembly of a single coordinating metaphor: the sense of the season as a beautiful but fatally fragile equilibrium. The rich configuration of absolute fullness that originally dominates the ode "To Autumn" is itself oxymoronic: perfect fulfillment can only portend decay. The year's harvest is the year's continental divide, the end of its triumph and the beginning of its defeat. With this light borrowed from the closing stanza, we can begin to uncover the long sequence of explicit signal images that have pointed at the poem's theme from the beginning.

In addition to the generic threat of decay in fruition, we now sense the whispered menace of "they think warm days will never cease" and the dark ambiguities of "o'er-brimmed" and "clammy cells." In the second stanza these impressions crowd upon us: in all the soundless, patient passivity of the personified figure; in all the ramified images of "hook" and harvest; in the narcotic somnolence of the heavy sweetness of odors; in all the multiplied finalities of sound and image. Reflect for a moment, in this connection, on the almost inexhaustible connotativeness of lines like these:

> Or by a cyder-press, with patient look,
> Thou watchest the last oozings hours by hours.

But all these data, all these impressions, are miraculously caught up in the great simple image of the gleaner who "dost keep / Steady thy laden head across a brook." In that figure, walking level, gliding, fulfilled, calmly toward the death of the year, we have the embodiment of the tragic sense of life: what she carries on her head in serene balance is the burden of the Mystery; where she walks is the high table land of Keats's full maturity of spirit and of art.

I have tried to show the complex sources of the poem's effect; but the effect itself is not complicated. That in a way is the heart of the matter—the simple oneness that results from all the complication. This special poised peace is the theme of the poem; it is what the poem exists to say and it says it by mood and tone and by those brilliantly passive images of the gleaner. We do have to keep coming back to those. What they dramatize is something like catharsis—all passion not spent but reconciled, sublimated, held in philosophical equipoise. The poem says these things within the scheme of the odes as a whole and also within its own proper boundaries. If we think of the odes as a sequence, this ode is their proper terminus in dynamic peace. Thematically it is immeasurably richer than it has been held to be. That the ode is a "nature poem," as is so often said, is true only in a kindergarten sense. Far from ignoring the conventional mythic and poetic associations of autumn, as some say Keats has done, he exploits exactly that fullest conventional significance with naked originality.

Murry was quite right when he called this a perfect poem; it is one of the species that defines the genus. It is poetry of the order that Keats called "great & unobtrusive." It is the quality of these odes that makes one more and more certain that Keats is the poet from the nineteenth century who is to satisfy our notions of the wholly valuable, the near ancestor for whom we feel most grateful, the one who best meets the mendicant eye asking passion and grace, susceptibility and manliness, news of art and life.

The View from the Side

I

The Education of Henry Adams is a work of such subtlety and sophistication that it is hard to believe it was written by an American—written, at that, a good forty years before we all got so complicated and clever. For beauty of thought and style, for authentic difficulty, earned density of matter and manner, I can think of nothing to compare with it but the greatest novels of Henry James, and even they are finally less resistant and elusive. "Words are slippery and thought is viscous," Adams remarks on page 451,[1] when we are long past the need to be told. It is important to remember that James and Adams were friends, that they were doing their finest and most complex work at exactly the same time, in the first years of the new century; and it is some comfort to see that William James, brother to one and friend to both, found reading them hard to the point of exasperation.

In talking of his book, as in talking of his life in his book, Adams adopted the pose of failure. When he completed his manuscript early in 1907 he had forty copies printed privately, then another sixty copies, to be sent about to friends for judgment and revision. He invited his friends, especially those mentioned in the book, to cut and slash and emend at will. He kept saying that the book had fallen so far short of his hopes that he was more than half inclined to suppress it altogether; and indeed he never brought it out himself, though he did authorize a posthumous edition in the copyright of the Massachusetts Historical Society, and that was published by Houghton Mifflin in 1918. In letters accompanying the privately circulated copies Adams applied a humorous rhetoric of hyperbolical deprecation. "The *Education* . . . is a picture of my aphorism that it is impossible to underrate human intelligence—beginning with one's own," he wrote to Margaret Chanler. "I am ashamed of it, and send it out into the world only to be whipped." To William James he described himself as "the champion failer of all" and lamented that he had been

---

[1] My text is the Riverside Edition (Boston: Houghton Mifflin, 1973), beautifully edited by Ernest Samuels. I am greatly indebted to Mr. Samuels's annotations.

able to carry his design only far enough to "see the impossibility of success." Both Jameses were too intelligent not to admire Adams's *Education*. Neither the life nor the book is a failure. One can see the sense in which, by Adams's supernal standards, neither is a success; but surely by any reasonable moral or aesthetic measure both are intricate and beautiful. I judge the *Education* to be the single book of highest distinction ever produced by an American.

Ordinarily in dealing with a work of literature the first problem is to find a handle to turn the work about so as to measure its achievement against its ambition. In dealing with the *Education* the most obvious handle, and one we dare not let go, is the phenomenon of one's bafflement, the book's unique combination of slipperiness of language—its quicksilver style—and viscosity or profundity of thought: its density of ideas and its immense range of learning, within which the voice of Adams moves with an elegant elliptical allusiveness, a kind of tough dandyism of mind, at once lofty, fastidious, and robust. In fact Adams is far more seeming-candid than most writers in offering himself for manipulation: handles stick out all round his work, as in that crazy sentence-making machine that Gulliver finds in the Academy of Lagado. All of his statements of design are helpful in some degree, even when they border on disingenuousness.

To William James he described the book as a piece of intellectual therapy, written like his *Mont-Saint-Michel and Chartres* "to clean off a bit of the surface of my mind . . . always to clean my own mind." In writing to his dear friend Charles Milnes Gaskell of Wenlock Abbey in Shropshire, Adams first described his *Education* offhandedly as "my last Will and Testament," but he went on to speak of something more fundamental, his outright elegiac motive: "The volume is wholly due to piety on account of my father and John Hay." In a second letter to Gaskell a few days later he remarked that if he published his book, "I shall have survived, buried, and praised my friends, and shall go to sleep myself. *It is time.*" He was in his sixty-ninth year, but he had been feeling, or at any rate talking, like an old man for a good many years. The elegiac is a dominant note in the *Education*, one of its most resonant and affecting.

Equally affecting is Adams's wish to write a helpful book, of service particularly to young persons seeking a way to an education that will help them to plan and conduct a life in the terrifying "multiplicity" of the new century. His own "failures" were to be exemplary and monitory, to help, as he put it in his 1907 preface, "to fit young men, in universities or elsewhere, to be men of the world, equipped for any emergency." An extravagant hope for any education, surely, but always pragmatical in impulse. To Gaskell he presented his volume more simply and touchingly as a kind of emeritus performance of a failed Harvard professor of history and failed historian of contemporary affairs: "my closing lectures to undergraduates in the instruction abandoned and broken off in 1877." Deadly serious in his aim to contribute to a reform in education, particularly in the teaching and learning of history, he intended to circulate his book, accompanied by his long supplementary essay, "The Rule of Phase Applied to History," at large among American teachers of history. This scheme was later abandoned.

Adams's address to an intended audience of students may remind one of Thoreau's remark in the second paragraph of *Walden*: "Perhaps these pages are more particularly addressed to poor students." Benjamin Franklin had undertaken his *Autobiography* in 1771 in the form of a letter to his son, to tell a story of a successful and happy life, possibly "fit to be imitated"; and he picked it up again in 1784, he says, on the urging of friends such as Benjamin Vaughan who admired what they had seen of his account of "the manners and situation of a rising people" and of a personal life that might "induce more men to spend lives fit to be written." Adams himself cites Franklin as his American predecessor in presenting a memoir as a "model . . . of self-teaching." Franklin's book is a small classic, nourishing and charming, but it reads like a primer alongside *The Education of Henry Adams*.

The models Adams mentions repeatedly are the confessions of St. Augustine and Jean-Jacques Rousseau, though he considers both of them ultimately failures, going awash in metaphysics and egotism respectively. If Adams wishes his *Education* to be exemplary and monitory, the self is his necessary subject, but he seeks at all costs to avoid the traps of the ego. He resorts to all sorts of self-distancing and self-diminishing devices, such as the clothes metaphor he borrows from *Sartor Resartus*, by which he becomes the Teufelsdröckh of his own tale, a "lay-figure" or "manikin" who (or which) is to be "taken for real" and "treated as though it had life" ("Who knows?" says Adams; "Possibly it had!"), as it rickets about in the "garment" of its education to show forth to students "the faults of the patchwork fitted on their fathers." This resolve to avoid self-celebration comes near to taking command of the book, both matter and manner, dictating basic decisions in regard to point of view, selection, emphasis, tone, language itself.

We must see that Adams judges the failures of Augustine and Jean-Jacques to be failures of art, for his own ambition was consciously literary: he wished to work not primarily as historian or as biographer but as artist. Augustine alone among memoirists, he thought, had possessed a genuine "idea of literary form,—a notion of writing a story with an end and object, not for the sake of the object, but for the form, like a romance," and he failed because he could not sustain his conceived artistic shape, his drama. Adams's own purpose and his own failure had been of the same order, he felt when he had finished, or abandoned, his manuscript. He had written his *Mont-Saint-Michel and Chartres* and his *Education*, he told Edith Morton Eustis, not in order "to teach others, but to educate myself in the possibilities of literary form." He went on: "Between artists, or people trying to be artists the sole interest is that of form. . . . The arrangement, the construction, the composition, the art of climax are our only serious study." We note the personal possessive pronoun. He wrote William James that the *Education* "interests me chiefly as a literary experiment, hitherto, as far as I know, never tried or never successful," and he went on to specify the kinship of art he felt with Henry James: "Your brother Harry tries such experiments in literary art daily, and would know instantly what I mean." When he wrote Henry James on May 6, 1908, he addressed him with jocular geniality as *frater*.

In his only reference in the *Education* to James's novels, Adams remarks that "Henry James had not yet [in 1862] taught the world to read a volume for the pleasure of seeing the lights of his burning-glass turned on alternate sides of the same figure." In 1908 he saw himself as having joined James in such experiments and failed at the enterprise. In a letter to his dear friend Elizabeth Cameron he made another crucial use of his metaphor of light and angle of view. He was being tempted to publish his *Education*, he said, chiefly as a way to avoid the pressure of demands that he do an outright memoir of John Hay: "All memoirs lower the man in estimation." He wished instead to give Hay a just elevation, and the best device for that was some such elliptical view as the *Education* employed: "Such a side light is alone artistic." Adams's light would not be a burning-glass but something more shifting, shaded, and oblique.

Perhaps Adams's most helpful comments in the letters surrounding the *Education* have to do with its structure, "the arrangement, the construction, the composition"—what James would have called *ordonnance*. In writing to Barrett Wendell, for example, Adams links himself cheerfully with Augustine and Rousseau as failers in an enterprise of impossible difficulty: "We have all three undertaken to do what cannot be successfully done—mix narrative and didactic purpose and style." I take the grammar of the latter clause to imply not two counters but three: story, argument, style. He, Augustine, and Rousseau had all attempted the "*tour-de-force* of writing drama with what is essentially undramatic."

Yet Adams feels that his task was the hardest of the three, and his failure perhaps the least shaming, owing to the greater perplexity for an American in trying to find and fix a satisfactory "atmosphere." To Elizabeth Cameron he also described his struggle "to keep an atmosphere." The idea is complex and none too clear as Adams applies it. By the term itself he probably meant what we more commonly call context or background, and he used the latter term to William James: "It is the old story of an American drama. You can't get your contrasts and backgrounds." With more than a dozen volumes of American history, biography, and fiction behind him, Adams presumably knew what he was talking about. But why was an American atmosphere or background so hard to fix? He leaves us to sort the matter out for ourselves. My assumption is that he had in mind the relative thinness, the lack of density and definition, the something anarchic and formless in our culture, its reluctance to take shapes and hold them, our heterogeneousness and our lingering infantilism, our way of growing bigger and older without growing up, the shifting baby-fat that keeps moving under the national skin.

To describe the structure of his book in the usual sense of order, proportion, scope, Adams offered a typically amusing and intricate figure in a letter to James Ford Rhodes:

> If you can imagine a centipede moving along in twenty little sections (each with a mathematical formula carefully concealed in his stomach) to the bottom of a hill; and then laboriously climbing in fifteen sections more (each with a new mathematical formula carefully concealed in its stomach) till it can get up on a hill an inch or two high, so as to see ahead a half inch or so, you will understand in advance all that the "Education" has to say.

This is Adams's way of saying that his book moves in a system of twenty chapters, about three hundred pages, carrying his story from "Quincy" in 1838 to "Failure" in 1871 (the bottom of the hill); then, after a startling hiatus in the narrative, a further fifteen chapters, about two hundred pages, moving from "Twenty Years After" in 1892 to "Nunc Age" in 1905.

In reading one comes slowly and perhaps sullenly to recognize that Adams is a good deal less interested in "narrative" than in "didactic purpose." Particularly after he breaks off his story abruptly in 1871, there is less and less narrative, more and more abstraction, speculation, philosophical postulating. A book that willfully leaps over twenty years in the life of its "subject" can hardly call itself a Life: Adams's own proposed subtitle was "A Study of Twentieth-Century Multiplicity." He meant what he said when he called the central persona a manikin and a lay-figure. In the later chapters especially the light strikes more and more from the side; the lay-figure scarcely moves in body. What moves, ever more boldly and subtly, is the mind inside.

One may feel the emphases of the book as divided, elusive, even evasive; still Adams plays basically fair in the matter of the superior weight he will assign to argument. Writing to William James he pretended to have practiced a sleight of hand: trusting, he says, to the smallness and inattentiveness of his audience, he had "hid" in the last hundred pages of *Mont-Saint-Michel and Chartres* "a sort of anchor in history"; then in the *Education*, conceived as "a companion study of the twentieth century," he had proceeded to "hide" a supplementary hundred pages of historical theory in the midst of "a stack of rubbish meant only to feed the foolish." This is to scoff at his reader and at four-fifths of his own book: his hyperboles can be merely exasperating. To Henry James he put the case more plainly: the *Education* was conceived as "a completion and mathematical conclusion from the previous volume about the Thirteenth Century,—the three concluding chapters of this being only a working out to Q.E.D. of the three concluding chapters of that." Not only in letters but in his prefaces and in his main text, Adams kept trying to make clear that his subject was not The Life of Henry Adams but the failure of a figure called Henry Adams to accumulate an education requisite for living in the real world, the world that the historian must understand or at least chronicle honestly. The manikin is used, he says in his 1907 preface, because he is indispensable "for the study of relation."

Yet "the object of study," he insists, "is the garment, not the figure." In the ventriloquizing "Editor's Preface" which he wrote in 1916 to appear over the signature of Henry Cabot Lodge in the 1918 public edition, Adams called the *Education* a "sequel" to *Mont-Saint-Michel and Chartres*, always designed as such, and went on to quote the paragraph concluding chapter 29 that specifies such a relationship. The poor thing had failed, he lamented, because the author had not been able to master his literary form, especially at the end: "Probably he was . . . trying only to work into it his favorite theory of history."

But it is high time to try to observe Adams's mingled purposes of story, argument, style going about their business of forming the work of art at which he professed to have failed. If this is failure, one must finally ask of the art as of the life, then what on earth is success?

II

The dominance of the didactic accumulates slowly, intensifying and spreading until at the end it almost entirely displaces other motives. Yet the didactic is not what first catches the eye, though it is quietly at work from the beginning. It seems absurd to say of a work that is in some sense autobiographical that it is self-conscious; but the self-consciousness of the *Education* is a special genus, born of didactic intention. This is not the ordinary self of autobiography, free like Whitman's self to lean and loaf at its ease, casually free to report its own doing, in whatever order of feeling, thought, and action. Adams's self is constrained by its function as exemplar, a datum, a proof in an argument, a figure in a demonstration.

This motive, not modesty actual or posed, directs the crucial decision to speak of the self always in the third person, to say not "I" but "he" or "Adams." The effects of such a simple device are complex and startling. Logically the third person, by distancing, ought to objectify; and Adams would justify it on those grounds, or pretend to do so. But it does not work that way in the *Education*: it abstracts, but it does not objectify. The self is not so much set off in a middle distance as set slightly to one side, while the writer's observing eye looks on with an obliqueness merely assumed or fictional. The abstracting effect of the third-person eye and voice works curiously to intensify rather than to diminish self-consciousness: we are always aware of the self self-consciously avoiding self-consciousness in order to posit a self that is merely phenomenal. The conception is fiendishly artful, so superbly managed that one is not only caught but deeply moved—by the motive as well as by the art.

Furthermore the third-person angle of narration contributes profoundly to the elegiac effect that richly pervades the whole book. We are always aware that it is old man Adams who has chosen to make a manikin of the self and set it to mime its way through a disenchanting, even humiliating demonstration, and who looks back over the pathetic phases of its failure across a span of seventy years with a reminiscent irony, an eye that is disappointed and resigned but also indulgent, amused, grateful.

The discovery of how good Adams is at the novelist's craft of narrative, character, atmosphere makes one lament his decision to throw his main force on the side of historical argument, and it may make one feel the more surly about struggling with the intricacies of the argument itself. The discovery occurs early, for in his first chapters, particularly in his first pages, Adams does some of the best pure writing ever produced in this country.

The long first chapter, "Quincy (1838–1848)," is brilliant in local vividness and suggested range, and it contains the whole book in miniature. It sets moving the master metaphor fundamental to the book's habit of artifice: the figure of life as a "game" which Adams never quite joined as a player because he "lost himself in the study of it"—characteristically a study mainly of the "errors" of the players. Failure is foreknown; the autumnal melancholy of the tale to come is forefelt. The "detached" third-person point of view is assumed from the beginning: a male child is born in February 1838 in the shadow of Boston State House. But Adams does not pretend that this "he," this "ten pounds of unconscious babyhood," is an Everybaby. This is not just any manikin but one with a name that entails a destiny. "It's a complex fate, being an American," wrote Henry James, who also described himself as "a citizen of the James family." Adams was an American, a New Englander, an Adams—all being forms of fate, as he is superbly aware. He is born into "a nest of association so colonial—so troglodytic"; in church on Sunday the boy reads, over the bald head of his grandfather President John Quincy Adams, the plaque in memory of his great-grandfather President John Adams. "You'll be thinkin' you'll be President too," the Irish gardener says to him sardonically. (Not everyone has an Irish gardener.) The boy is surprised at the doubt implied in the statement.

The early omens are dubious. He belongs to the third generation after President John, he is the youngest of three brothers, and a severe attack of scarlet fever in his fourth year turns him into the runt of the litter: he "fell behind his brothers two or three inches in height, and proportionally in bone and weight." The effect upon his "character and processes of mind," Adams suggests tentatively, may have been a certain "fining-down process of scale," and an intensification of his natural inclination to the New Englander's critical cast of mind: "The habit of doubt; of distrusting his own judgment and of totally rejecting the judgment of the world; the tendency to regard every question as open; the hesitation to act except as a choice of evils; the shirking of responsibility; the love of line, form, quality; the horror of ennui; the passion for companionship and the antipathy to society." But Adams has no intention of presenting himself as neurasthenic. He remarks once that as a boy his nerves were "delicate" and that when he was older he "exaggerated" that weakness. He treats the matter frankly and drops it, and we hear hardly another word of nerves or health of any kind. He thinks of himself as "normal" and believes that others so regard him.

No, he insists, what is to be "peculiar" in his nature will be a function of "education," not "character"; and he gives us thus early a view of the complex things he will mean by his key term, a definition inclusive enough to carry us to the end of the long book: "From cradle to grave this problem of running order through chaos, direction through space, discipline through freedom, unity through multiplicity, has always been, and must always be, the task of education, as it is the moral of religion, philosophy, science, art, politics, and economy." What he has described is his whole permanent field of attention. In these early pages Adams gives us as well the decisive first datum in the education, his grounding, blood and bones, in the blunt and beautiful rhythm of New England seasons, which he sets in a classical rhetorical frame of comparison and contrast: the long cold white winter in which the earth seems to die and men and animals stumble about like somnambular spirits, followed by the shockingly sudden and complete resurrection of the miraculous green world in the "drunken" summer. Adams uses the seasonal cycle brilliantly, as fact and trope: "The double exterior nature gave life its relative values. Winter and summer, cold and heat, town and country, force and freedom, marked two modes of life and thought, balanced like lobes of the brain." A sensitive boy who grows up in New England weather takes the lesson of bifurcation into his tissues: "life was double."

Already we begin to sense the basic strategy of the book, as much a matter of temperament as of design, adopted more or less helplessly because it is its author's cast of mind. The discipline of dividedness, of ambiguity, the sense of duality as the habit of fact as of perception pervades this first chapter, and it will grow ever more beautiful and baffling. As summer and country are set against winter and town, so freedom is set against constraint, youth against age, moral and political Adamses against banking Brookses: Grandfather John Quincy Adams gives Bibles; Grandfather Peter Chardon Brooks gives silver mugs. Grandmother Louisa Catherine Johnson Adams, "the Madam," embodies dividedness: half English and half American, dragged about the capitals of the world by chances of war and politics, settled at last in a colonial house with Queen Anne paneling and Louis Seize furniture, in old age in the middle of the American nineteenth century she still seems lost. It is no wonder that Henry Adams should trace to her a strain of ambivalence in his genetic equipment: "those doubts and self-questionings, those hesitations."

For Adams the crucial dividedness is temporal. By heritage, by temperament, by moral, political, and aesthetic inclination, he feels himself to be a throwback to an age already dead, "a child of the eighteenth century." Yet before he is six he has seen the twentieth century foretold by the railroad, the steamship, the telegraph, and it is a citizen of the twentieth century who tells the whole story of the *Education*. By the end he has worked his way through to a humorous and reluctant peace: old Henry Adams has just discovered that the best way to follow the track of the Virgin in French medieval stained glass is by motor car. It was the nineteenth century, the real arena of his living, with which Adams could never make peace. "He never could compel himself to care for nineteenth-century style," he remarks laconically in his first chapter. The temper that set him against the temper of his time, so that he never willingly inhabited his life, freed him to play the revenant, the alien and skeptical sojourner.

At one early point Adams appears flatly to deny any such alienation. He says roundly: "To his life as a whole he was a consenting, contracting party and partner from the moment he was born to the moment he died." But the whole weight and coloring of the story as it accumulates show the disingenuousness of the statement. He is trying to protect the fiction of the representativeness of his Henry Adams manikin, whose exemplary function works only if he is accepted as a "consciously assenting member" of his age. The more illuminating metaphor is his conventional life-game figure. Adams had been, originally, willing to play the game of his age, to contend for plums and power within its cynical rules, and he knew the cards he held were the strongest; but instead of playing he "lost himself in study" of the game, as he says. It was "failure" that turned him into a suave Thersites: spectator, learned student, critic, and ironical chronicler of a bitter comedy. Hence that persistent light from the side.

Adams's obsessive theme of personal failure is hyperbolical and to an irritating degree perverse—at once self-indulgent and self-flagellant, almost masturbatory—but it is more than a mere trope. By the measure of his own very large ambitions for worldly power (to be exercised, of course, with Adams and eighteenth-century highmindedness) he was indeed established early as a failure. But the age fails with him, far more consequentially, and it is in his function as critic that Adams is a "consenting member" of the public process. Consent need not imply applause. Yet along the way to failure Adams does find much to praise in the way of human performance: hence the profound and touching effect of elegy and eulogy in the *Education*.

His early perception of life as double is the primitive movement in the definition of education as a struggle to "run" order through chaos, unity through multiplicity. The definition, formed in study and experience, is both cause and effect of Adams's Hegelian habit of mind which finds antithesis everywhere set against thesis; but it is moral and intellectual energy that impels the mind to drive toward ever higher synthesis. The highest synthesis, the highest knowable truth, presumably must be an affair of tone, the shade into which all the warring opposites finally coalesce. The very first sensuous experience Adams can remember is a kind of absolute, unshaded: a child of three sitting on a yellow-painted kitchen floor in a patch of hard sunlight. The characteristic quality of New England light was "glare": "The boy was a full man before he ever knew what was meant by atmosphere. . . . After a January blizzard, the boy who could look with pleasure into the violent snow-glare of the cold white sunshine, with its intense light and shade, scarcely knew what was meant by tone." Knowledge of tone was to be reached "only by education." *The Education of Henry Adams* is ultimately a triumph of the achievement of tone, in the most ramified sense: tone as knowledge, tone as commensurate style.

III

"Failure" is the twentieth section of his down-slanted "centipede" of structure, and it closes the long first movement of the book. Adams extends the chapter through an account of the summer following his first year of teaching, chiefly to include his first meeting with Clarence King, presented as a benign crisis in his own history, a rounding and closing of a long phase of education and a beginning of "life." Adams had traveled west as a "friend of geologists" to take a spectator's part with one of the field parties of the Fortieth Parallel Survey which was mapping the geology of a hundred-mile-wide belt along the line of the newly completed Union Pacific Railroad. Such a gesture of the still disheveled young republic seeking definition of itself was bound to appeal to Adams for its transcendental quality, and bound to strike him as symbolically right to produce, at its western terminus, Henry Adams on a solitary mule, belated and lost, stumbling through the dark in a canyon of Estes Park to discover Clarence King in a lamplit Rocky Mountain cabin. It won't do to smile at this kind of thing: fate is fate, and we must grant a sufficiently poetical mind its right to play. A Dantesque density surrounds the meeting of Adams and the gay, paradoxical, star-crossed young man of such preternatural charm and high capacity; and though beyond this point King is only flickeringly visible in the book, like Charles Francis Adams and John Hay and the literally invisible Marian Hooper Adams he is a resident ghost, a shade enriching its mysterious and beautiful texture.

The most astonishing of Adams's elaborate strategies of structure is a negative act: the decision to leave a gap of a full twenty years in his narrative. The hiatus occurs not in the act of writing but in the stuff of the book, the material of the narrative. Adams does not set his task aside for many years and then pick it up again where he left off, as Franklin did; his writing was quite swift and continuous, most of it done in 1904–1905, and within that process he decided to leave the hiatus—as a structural member of the work, a design of ellipsis. It was a bold decision and at first glance a perverse one, the coarsest of Adams's perversities. What staggers the reader is that what he chooses to pass over are his twenty years of "success," the years when he was "doing his work," when he was most fully "living" by an ordinary measure of biographical matter. It is not easy to think of any other autobiographer who so resolutely turns his back when he might have been puffing out his chest.

The case is less absolute than I am making it sound. Adams has already shown us a summary sketch of his career as teacher and editor, and that carries us to 1877. And in "Twenty Years After," in a still more sketchy and elliptical treatment, he does tell us what he had "done" in the interval down to 1892: with Grant off the scene and W. M. Evarts and Hay in the State Department, Adams had gone back to Washington to be a "stable-companion to statesmen, whether they liked it or not," and to "write history"; in fifteen years or so he had produced an "altogether ridiculous" number of printed volumes. But such vague laconicisms encompass an enormous willed reticence. The "altogether ridiculous" formula, for example, covers the most varied and distinguished canon of his generation—not only the monumental nine-volume *History of the United States during the Administrations of Jefferson and Madison*, but also two volumes of biography, a collection of historical essays, and two stylish and original novels to which Adams never even put his name. He pretends to no impact on the culture of the day; like Henry James's Dencombe in "The Middle Years," he says he had "worked in the dark," and Adams reckons only three "serious readers": Abram Hewitt, Wayne McVeagh, and John Hay.

The largest and most moving of these withholdings is Adams's refusal to speak at all of his marriage—thirteen happy years from 1872 to 1885 with Marian Hooper Adams in Cambridge, Washington, and Europe, terminated by her suicide in a period of deep depression following the death of her father. The closest Adams comes to any reference to his wife or his marriage is the enigmatic paragraph at the end of "Twenty Years After," as hooded and haunting as Saint-Gaudens's memorial figure itself, his brooding communion with which in the spring of 1892 recalls another Henry James situation—Marcher at the end of "The Beast in the Jungle." Adams is expressing, by his withholding, what Ernest Samuels calls his "somber pose" that he had died when his wife died: her death "broke his life in halves," as he wrote elsewhere; and the second half of his life, as of his book, is "posthumous" in feeling, a ghost's drifting reverie. But indeed her unmentioned death colors the whole book, and is the profoundest source of its elegiac feeling. Surely we need look little farther for the psychology of the twenty-year hiatus. Adams could not talk in detail of the period without talking of his marriage, and he could not bear to talk of it.

Odd as it may seem to go on at such length about something that is not present in the work being examined, in dealing with the *Education* one needs to work in the spirit of Stevens's Snow Man, who wished to attend not only to "nothing that is not there" but also to "the nothing that is." When an autobiographer chooses to pass over the twenty most productive years of his life, he creates a negation that is a phenomenon in itself, a nothing that is. The missing marriage is a negation within the negation, and if its beauty and grievousness largely explain the emotional logic of omission, the logic of literary tactics needs to be sought elsewhere. The primary fact, as he himself insists, is that Adams is not really writing autobiography in the ordinary sense. His renewed insistence, in exclamatory form, in the opening sentence of chapter 21, "Twenty Years After," carries something of the force of the reinvocation of the Muse as Spenser or Milton or Pope draws a deep breath for the last movement of epical action: "Once more! this is a story of education, not of adventure!" He now carefully restates his purpose: "It is meant to help young men—or such as have intelligence enough to seek help—but it is not meant to amuse them." The *Education* is more a pragmatic philosophical treatise than it is an autobiography, and Adams now ceremonially redefines "education" for the "barely one man in a hundred" who "owns a mind capable of reacting to any purpose on the forces that surround him": "The object of education for that mind should be the teaching itself how to react with vigor and economy. . . . Education should try to lessen the obstacles, diminish the friction, invigorate the energy, and should train minds to react, not at haphazard, but by choice, on the lines of force that attract their world."

If I understand his grammar, by "reacting to any purpose on" he means "to influence, to work usefully upon." Hence an account of the uses to which he put his education would seem to be very much in point. But Adams is already committed to presenting his education as failure, and so he has had to ignore twenty years of productive "life" in order to avoid the skewing effect of success. This tactic, in combination with his definition above, involves him in another paradox. What matters is action, yet what Adams "did" with his education is not the "inquirer's" proper concern: "It is a personal matter which would only confuse him." The inquirer who would have enjoyed an opportunity to be confused by all that personal matter must make the best of his deprivation. It would have been one thing, sufficiently cynical, if Adams had chosen directly to apply the label of failure to his twenty years of marriage, publication, and stable-companionship with statesmen. Perhaps the case is that he could have validated such a view only by treating his wife's suicide as decisive; and though that may indeed have been his deepest feeling, the event itself is for him literally unspeakable.

Adams picks up his narrative, in the increasingly vague sense in which he is writing narrative, at a point of low vitality: "Education had ended in 1871 [when he 'began to apply it for practical uses like his neighbors']; life was complete in 1890; the rest mattered so little!" After twenty years of concentrated work, he had "thought his own duties sufficiently performed and his account with society settled." He has "enjoyed his life amazingly," but it seems to him essentially finished, and in any case he is tired and low in nervous energy, so he has simply broken things off. Now, nearing fifty-four years of age in January 1892, he lies glooming in a London hospital after a minor operation. He had just "come up from the South Seas with John La Farge"—a phrase that covers more than a year of travel with his painter friend. It is a bit dashing to be told, with twenty-five years, fifteen chapters, two hundred pages still to go, that life is over and what remains matters little; but one has learned by now to play these games with Adams, to fall into sympathy with his mood and manner, and to await rewards with confidence.

One has now come face to face, I think, with the crux of Adams's artistic problem at which he thought he had failed: how to make "dramatic," or shapely and interesting, material that is essentially undramatic—as he has resolved to limit it. After this point narrative virtually disappears. In effect Adams almost ceases to act visibly; he moves, driftingly, from place to place, but his basic action goes on in the mind, as thought—observation, speculation, formulation. As the narrative energy diminishes, the philosophical energy intensifies, the texture of thought and speech grows ever more dense, the whole enterprise more complex, more interesting or less interesting according to taste. Even in the "posthumous" phase of his life, Adams has not ceased to live a rich personal life, though it is blighted by his widowerhood and then by his hopeless attachment to Elizabeth Cameron, wife of his friend in the Senate. Hence, though he has now chosen to act by thinking, he also acts by feeling. His way of expressing feeling is classical in kind—reticent, elliptical, underspecified, suggestive; but the feeling itself is so rich, so strong, so intelligent that it takes subterranean control of the book and of one's responses to it.

Adams's education did not cease in 1871, any more than his life ended in 1890. Both continue for the whole span of the book, to 1905—and beyond. But direction and emphasis, the rhythm of energy, change in the education as in the life. When the life has moved into the mind, it is too late to train oneself for effective action or reaction upon "the lines of force that attract [one's] world." Education also moves into the mind, to become a sifting and sorting and formulating, an effort to set things straight in their patterns. It is, personally, an appeasement of the mind's hunger for order, and, less personally, a powerful continuing tutorial urge, a desire to transmit a body of insight that will free younger men to act with more intelligence and less waste.

Henry Adams was blessed with one of the richest of human gifts, a genius for friendship, and surely no man of his day possessed a larger, warmer, or more brilliant circle of friends of both sexes. Persons of high gifts themselves, of his own age and also younger, enjoyed his company and treasured his affection and approval. As a houseguest or traveling companion he was welcomed for weeks or months at a stretch by men like King, La Farge, Saint-Gaudens and by families such as the Camerons, the Lodges, the Hays, the Roosevelts. His own talk was copious, witty, full of meat, as were his letters. The *Education* itself makes none of these claims; it simply cites occasions whose mere recurrence proves the case.

Adams and John Hay had had the exquisite satisfaction of building adjoining houses in Lafayette Square in Washington in 1884–1885, designed by Adams's good friend Henry Hobson Richardson, probably the finest of American Victorian architects; but Marian Adams had hardly lived to occupy her house, and after her death Henry Adams spent as much time in travel or residence abroad, especially in Paris, as he spent in Washington. His journeys were so numerous and so adventitious, and his account of them so systematically sidelong and impressionistic, that it is pointless to try to follow them. The journeys were social and intellectual in function, like the whole action of Adams's life now, and it is really the intricate movement of his mind that one must try to follow— dazzled, confused, and profoundly impressed by the almost arrogant masterliness of flight as a mind launches, soars, dives, hovers, perches, launches again. The whole of that flight is far too wide and complex to review; every reader must give himself the pleasure and the exasperation of following it for himself. A mere outline is task enough.

IV

The hazy autumnal atmosphere of this long final movement is suggested by characteristic chapter headings: "Silence," "Indian Summer," "Twilight," "Vis Inertiae," "Nunc Age." Autumn, Adams writes of the season itself, should be "a little sunny and a little sad." His own autumn is more sad than sunny, and we can feel the soreness of his heart within the tone of his beautifully stylized gaiety. The passing of time, and of friends, is a part of it, naturally, and Adams names his own age almost every year as he moves from his middle forties to his late sixties. A newly authentic sense of failure colors the mood as well. Adams's life now does really feel in a sense "posthumous." The persons he has loved most are dead, or otherwise unreachable, or failing along with him. He has put his work behind him: it is well enough in its way, but sadly limited in outreach for a boy who had dreamed of "controlling power in some form." He confesses in his understated way his sense of the irony of the fact that no public office has ever been offered to him, but he has put away the ambition to be a public man and the deprivation hardly seems to matter any more. What is left is ennui, restlessness, fear, and above all the passion of the mind to know before it dies—education in that desperate and beautiful sense. It is for that reason that the spectacle of life still matters, that the aging mind still drives itself to go over and over all it knows, and to keep on adding to its store.

Adams has not altogether given up his interest in politics and current affairs, but he watches such things now in a much more detached and musing spirit, as one datum among many in the huge design he is trying to puzzle out. He is on the track of the track of force, trying to understand the shape of the movement of power in time; he is more interested in the past and the future than in the present, though of course the present matters acutely as the most visible cusp in the graph of movement. The "honest historian," Adams remarks, must not take a partisan view of his data: "To him even the extinction of the human race should be merely a fact to be grouped with other vital statistics." He seemed now to care little what way national or international affairs drifted, except in the very personal sense that the reputation and even the health of John Hay as secretary of state were bound up with the drift. Adams describes himself, Hay, and Clarence King as "inseparable" after 1879, but King spends so much of his life "underground"—in the doubly punning sense of his mining operations and his secret common-law marriage to a black woman in New York—that he remains a shadow in the narrative, and it is Hay who matters most to Adams as a friend of the bosom, and hence to the reader. Adams views Hay's tenure as a triumph at the cost of life.

But the larger triumph of the quarter-century is the vast increase and "concentration" of mechanical power, and of the money-power that will manage and exploit it, the "banker's Olympus" of capitalism. As an honest historian Adams must be the fascinated recorder of that process; but he can take no pleasure in it, for it means the death of his class and of the eighteenth-century principles he has fought for all his life: "strict construction, limited powers, George Washington, John Adams, and the rest." This social and political death leaves Adams feeling "posthumous" in yet another sense, and farther and more scornfully distanced from the tide of affairs.

In his famous chapter 25, "The Dynamo and the Virgin," Henry Adams describes the habits of his guild: "Historians undertake to arrange sequences,—called stories, or histories—assuming in silence a relation of cause and effect. These assumptions, hidden in the depths of dusty libraries, have been astounding, but commonly unconscious and childlike." In the same rueful paragraph he sketches his own historian's history:

> Adams, for one, had toiled in vain to find out what he meant. He had even published a dozen volumes of American history for no other purpose than to satisfy himself whether, by the severest process of stating, with the least possible comment, such facts as seemed sure, in such order as seemed rigorously consequent, he could fix for a familiar moment a necessary sequence of human movement. The result had satisfied him as little as at Harvard College. Where he saw sequence, other men saw something quite different, and no one saw the same unit of measure.

The one thing he "insisted" on was "a relation of sequence," refusing to accept the anarchy of randomness: one thing must follow another not by chance but according to some motive, logic, shape, an order at least of energy if not of conscious design. To this hypothesized sequential energy of history he assigns the name *attraction*. He is willing to find it anywhere, but he insists on finding it somewhere: "The matter of direction seemed vital."

In the autumnal mood of his late years, "holding open the door into the next world," a "Teufelsdröckh," a "stranded Tannhäuser," a "dove of sixty years old, alone and uneducated, who has lost his taste even for olives," but still "passionately seeking education," Adams continues to study "his ignorance in silence." His historian's object is "to triangulate from the widest possible base to the furthest point he thinks he can see, which is always far beyond the curvature of the horizon." Seeking to widen his base, and to understand it newly, he spends months and years conning again his old knowledge and adding new. His aim is "to follow the track of the energy," or, reversing his figure, "to keep in front of the movement, and, if necessary, lead it to chaos, but never fall behind. Only the young have time to linger in the rear." Such an objective, he considered, was "not extravagant or eccentric. One sought no absolute truth. One sought only a spool on which to wind the thread of history without breaking it." Adams's thinking, phenomenally rangy and ingestive, comes to concentrate gradually on two main lines, finally a single line, a concept of force or power as religious as it is scientific.

The Dynamo and the Virgin, both so quiet, so chaste, so powerful, so mysterious, merge at last in the mind. Adams finds himself describing the Virgin as the "animated dynamo," implying reproduction and hence a principle of infinity. In the great gallery of machines at the Paris exposition of 1900, he "found himself lying . . . with his historical neck broken by the sudden irruption of forces totally new":

> He began to feel the forty-foot dynamos as a moral force, much as the early Christians felt the Cross. The planet itself seemed less impressive, in its old-fashioned, deliberate, annual or daily revolution, than this huge wheel, revolving within arm's-length at some vertiginous speed, and barely murmuring—scarcely humming an audible warning to stand a hair's-breadth further for respect of power—while it would not wake the baby lying close against its frame.

"Before the end," he continues, "one began to pray to it; inherited instinct taught the natural expression of man before silent and infinite force." One approaches the Dynamo, like the Virgin, with fear or love but certainly with respect: each is an "occult mechanism." I suppose one must conclude that Henry Adams ended up seeking God—though, looking down from his historian's Olympus, he will not thank one for saying so.

With his poetical rationalism, his superbly mortal intelligence, Adams had been in flight from religion all his life; but it did him no more good than it did Jonah, in Melville's phrase, "to flee world-wide from God." An implicit reverentness, sometimes nearly, reluctantly explicit, thickens and irradiates the long last movement of the *Education*. When the old student Henry Adams "imagines" himself three hundred years old in a sixteenth-century French church, "kneeling before the Virgin's window in the silent solitude of an empty faith, crying his culp, beating his breast, confessing his historical sins, weighed down by the rubbish of sixty-six years' education, and still desperately hoping to understand," he means to project a hyperbolical persona, bitterly humorous; but it is hard to mistake the rich sympathy for the image in the breast of the man who made it. The self scrutinizes itself rationally but with affectionate pity: the image is formed out of feeling too deep to accept burlesque.

The only religion Adams "professes"—after the great expositions of Chicago in 1893, Paris in 1900, and St. Louis in 1904—is "the religion of World's Fairs," by which he means his terrified attempt to understand and to "triangulate" the mighty new mechanical energies, the burly children of science at work on natural force. Chicago had seemed to Adams "the first expression of American thought as a unity," yet a thought that frightens and disgusts him, hardly thought at all but the more or less mindless elevation of mechanical power, with its necessary and equally offensive concomitants in politics and finance. In Paris his historical neck had been broken not only by the dynamos but by Röntgen rays, radium, and the internal combustion engine—occult mechanisms that seemed to imply anarchy, inscrutability in fundamental physical processes. By 1904 in St. Louis, the new American seemed to be confirmed as "the servant of the powerhouse, as the European of the twelfth century was the servant of the Church": he was "the child of steam and the brother of the dynamo."

V

Adams's concentration upon twin lines of force, spiritual/theological and mechanical/scientific, symbolized by the Virgin and the Dynamo, represented the culmination of a profoundly impressive discipline of scrutiny and rejection, too long—lifelong really but intensified in these final fifteen years—and too intricate to review here. His range and subtlety carried him not only deeply but repeatedly into history, of course, but also into politics, sociology, economics, psychology, literature, art, philosophy, and above all into theology and science, upon which bifurcation he may be said to have settled at last, more or less despairingly and by an act of will: "Satisfied that the sequence of men led to nothing and that the sequence of their society could lead no further, while the mere sequence of time was artificial, and the sequence of thought was chaos, he turned at last to the sequence of force." Seeking unity he had traveled continents and ransacked libraries and his own mind, and everywhere he had found only multiplicity. Even the line of natural force, which had hitherto seemed the one sure unity, was turning out under the new chemistry and physics to be as anarchic as the line of thought. What did appear certain was the vertiginous increase of power which, for its control and exploitation, was forcing society into modes of concentration at which Adams stared with pessimism and fastidious distaste.

His sense of reeling multiplicity everywhere about him drove Adams to join his young friend Bay Lodge in the "party" they called, only half humorously, the Conservative Christian Anarchists. With Hegel and Schopenhauer as patron saints, the little node of beleaguered intellectual aristocrats, acting on the great principle of contradiction, followed ideas from statement to dispersal to negation to reformulation, ad infinitum. Adams argued that "in the last synthesis, order and anarchy were one, but that the unity was chaos"; but then he reflected that he would be "equally obliged to deny the chaos." In a half-dozen of the most brilliant paragraphs in American writing he follows the tortuous track toward the higher synthesis and the "universal which thinks itself, contradiction and all." The moral of this desperate intellectual comedy is that the wholly serious mind can never satisfy itself, never rest; yet, if it is not to be merely paralyzed by ambivalence, it must force itself to pause and perch long enough to mine some limited area as deeply as it can penetrate. And so Adams's brain seizes the Virgin and the Dynamo and tosses them from lobe to lobe. He imagines himself as crawling like Sir Lancelot in the twelfth century along a knife-edge dividing "two kingdoms of force which had nothing in common but attraction"—their drive, energy, impact upon his own mind. The inscrutable "rays" that stood to him for the new science seemed "a revelation of mysterious energy like that of the Cross." Adams "made up his mind to venture it; he would risk translating rays into faith." In a sense, I suppose, he risks translating faith into rays, or science. His awe and love to go to the Virgin, his awe and fear to the Dynamo; his intellectual energy goes to both energies.

In the summer of 1895, when he visits twelfth- and thirteenth-century churches in Normandy, Caen, Coutances, Mont-Saint-Michel, in company with Mrs. Lodge and her two sons, the Virgin and the mysteries of faith begin to be resurrected for Adams's mind as powerful counters in the history of thought. Helped by these fresher minds to throw off the obscuring "German" bias lingering from his youth, he is awakened to a disturbing and seductive "new sense of history," an intuition of a strange and beautiful line of force that demands a new mode of understanding. But in the summer of 1899, alone in Paris and "hunted by ennui," he "entered the practice of his final profession" by undertaking a systematic survey, or "triangulation," of the twelfth century. In the late autumn John La Farge arrived on the scene, bringing his artist's and student's expertise in the stained glass in which the medieval men limned the images of their faith, as well as his bracing jibe "Adams, you reason too much!" Now Adams's study of the Virgin, particularly at Chartres, began to move in a more intuitive rhythm toward a point. To evoke the presence of La Farge the artist, Adams applies the glass-palette as fact and figure: "In conversation La Farge's mind was opaline with infinite shades and refractions of light, and with color toned down to the finest gradations. In glass it was insubordinate; it was renaissance; it asserted his personal force with depth and vehemence of tone never before seen."

Adams's "idol" Gibbon, in a phrase he quotes with hilarity, had "darted a contemptuous look on the stately monuments of superstition," the Gothic cathedrals. Adams's own look is baffled, awed, adoring, for the Virgin blends in his mind not only with Christ who is Love but with Venus who is Love again. She becomes Woman, sex, reproduction, the mysterious inspirer and continuator not only of faith but of the basic racial energy. After 1895, culminating a lifetime's admiration of Woman, Adams begins "to feel the Virgin or Venus as force"; she was "the highest energy ever known to man, the creator of four-fifths of his noblest art," and "all the steam in the world could not, like the Virgin, build Chartres." That seemed a kind of given, a historical fiat. But Adams is too honest to abandon either stream of force, faith or science, Virgin or Dynamo; and he must continue to live torn, like Adam in the garden, "between God who was unity, and Satan who was complexity."

The new physics had casually transformed "the scientific synthesis commonly called Unity" into "the scientific analysis commonly called Multiplicity. The two things were the same, all forms being shifting phases of motion." So rebuffed, the elderly seeker of Unity yearned simply to drop "the sounder into the abyss—let it go," hence to give up the chase entirely. Adams "saw his education complete, and was sorry he ever began it." It is the sense of the moral and political cynicism thickening around him that will not let him rest: "He repudiated all share in the world as it was to be, and yet he could not detect the point where his responsibility began or ended." Despairingly and bravely, he resolves simply to will a double concentration: he will face and study Multiplicity as a fact, and at the same time study the nearest thing to Unity he can see.

"Any schoolboy could see," as Adams puts it in one of his exasperating ritual phrases, that man "as a force" had to be measured "by motion, from a fixed point." For his fixed point he settled upon the century from 1150 to 1250, as expressed in the French cathedrals and the thought of Aquinas, as the period when men had felt most powerfully at least the illusion of Unity: "The point of history when man held the highest idea of himself as a unit in a unified universe." Beginning there, and working in philosophy and mechanics, he would attempt to "measure motion down to his own time without assuming anything as true or untrue, except relation," so to produce a volume to be called *Mont-Saint-Michel and Chartres: A Study of Thirteenth-Century Unity*. Thereafter, having fixed "a position for himself," he would confront twentieth-century Multiplicity in *The Education of Henry Adams*. With these two "points of relation" established, he could triangulate: "He hoped to project his lines forward and backward indefinitely, subject to correction from anyone who should know better." A bold program, surely, for a man of sixty-five. At past fifty Adams had "solemnly and painfully" learned to ride a bicycle. Now the double motives of his quest came together amusingly when the "elderly and timid single gentleman" bought an automobile, one of the new "nightmares" capable of a hundred kilometers an hour, and in such a juggernaut followed the track of the Virgin about France:

> For him, the Virgin was an adorable mistress, who led the automobile and its owner where she would, to her wonderful palaces and chateaux, from Chartres to Rouen, and thence to Amiens and Laon, and a score of others, kindly receiving, amusing, charming and dazzling her lover, as though she were Aphrodite herself, worth all else that man ever dreamed. He never doubted her force, since he felt it to the last fibre of his being, and could no more dispute its mastery than he could dispute the force of gravitation of which he knew nothing but the formula. He was only too glad to yield him-

self entirely, not to her charm or to any sentimentality of religion, but to her mental and physical energy of creation which had built up these World's Fairs of thirteenth-century force that turned Chicago and St. Louis pale.

Old Man Adams is wide awake to such conjunctions as comedy; yet the energy behind the enterprise was a despair so wide that it had to be defied if life was to continue. If in the most general sense Adams was seeking God (and finding mostly Satan), the thing he was fleeing was Self. Beyond all things he dreaded the final solipsism of being driven to the mind, his own mind, to find a locus of order or value—Unity. "Of all studies," he wrote, "the one he would rather have avoided was that of his own mind. He knew no tragedy so heartrending as introspection." Psychology had always seemed to him the least wholesome of his numerous sciences, and it is with pity and revulsion that he presents the figure of enlightened modern psychological man, the man who "knew" that "his normal condition was idiocy, or want of balance, and that his sanity was unstable artifice. His normal thought was dispersion, sleep, dream, inconsequence; the simultaneous action of different thought-centres without central control. His artificial balance was acquired habit. He was an acrobat, with a dwarf on his back, crossing a chasm on a slack-rope, and commonly breaking his neck." If the universe is to be "known only as motion of mind," and the property of mind is to "dissolve," then the condition of the serious seeker is heartrending indeed. It is at least in part with revulsion and defiance that Adams turns to the Virgin and the Dynamo: they are the creatures least like himself.

The turn is the act of a despairing yet indomitable intelligence, and there is great sadness in its resignation, as there is grandeur in its resoluteness. The man who had set out to know everything ends up wondering if anything is to be known. The direction of the turn has a great deal to do with both the form and the tone of the *Education*. The wish to move outside the self, to use it but not to depend upon it, not to live exclusively there, dictates the turn away from straight autobiography; the adoption of the view from the side in third-person narration turns the self into datum, a documentary or exemplary rather than a dramatic or even a subjective persona. The pessimism or resignation, the slow falling back from the dream, gives emotional and philosophical density to the elegiac mood of the whole book—which was written, after all, after these matters had been settled, for the most part sadly, in Adams's mind.

The long complex lines of thought, traced here so sketchily, fill perhaps two-thirds of the space in the final fifteen segments of Adams's centipede of structure. The rest of the space is occupied mainly by political affairs, noticed in large general international terms centering on the career of John Hay in the State Department, which Adams treats as a personal triumph that is ultimately suicidal. Adams's handling of the decline and death of Hay and King, so brief and so feeling as it is, sharpens the general autumnal air to a point of wintry chill. King, "the best and brightest man of his generation," goes first, late in 1901. For Adams there is comfort in the fact that he dies offstage, but a grinding wretchedness in contemplating the loneliness of his end in a California inn. Hay, who in Adams's view was killing himself in the country's service, lasts till 1905; and his death at Nauheim where Adams had just left him for rest and treatment is used by Adams to close his book, an event of implicit suicide beyond which he does not wish to speak: the rest is silence.

"Nunc Age"—Now Go—is his title for his last short chapter. "One walks with one's friends squarely up to the portal of life, and bids goodbye with a smile. One has done it so often!" Earlier Adams had remarked that "the affectation of readiness for death is a stage role, and stoicism is a stupid resource." But it was the only resource and Adams was reduced to it now. In its reticently eloquent way, the *Education* has been a paean to friendship all the way. Adams's rich quiet affectionateness is one of the book's primary sources of strength, as impressive as its cranky intellectual brilliance—though I wonder if it is any more moving. The book's triumph is compound and complex, a property of mind, of feeling, and of style.

THE HOUSE OF YEATS

It is now perfectly clear that William Butler Yeats is a classic, a man for all seasons, one of the great poets. T. S. Eliot described him generously but not extravagantly when he called him "the greatest poet of our time—certainly the greatest in this language, and so far as I am able to judge, in any language." Yeats may also have been a great man, though that is a harder judgment to make, and is perhaps not our business.

I wish to praise the poet under the title of "The House of Yeats." Under that roof, or umbrella, I am thinking of the house as the family, in the Greek sense, "the house of Atreus," for example, which bore the famous curse; also of Yeats's own deep familial or dynastic sense of himself and his origins; also of his feudal, courtly, aristocratic leanings, which need to be defined and qualified; finally of actual houses which in the course of his life accommodated him with an air of purpose and symbolism. I find my most inclusive text in a remark of Frank O'Connor's: "he was the most consistently noble man I have ever met." It is the nobility of Yeats, in its ramified and often surprising forms, that I wish to try to identify.

Confident as he was of his own creative gifts, Yeats never supposed that he had made himself; to be "self-born" (in his own phrase) was the privilege of gods or demons. Yeats was a Yeats, which is to say a union of Yeats and Pollexfen. It was his father who spoke what the poet called "the only eulogy that ever turned my head," as follows: "by marriage with a Pollexfen we have given a tongue to the sea cliffs." There is a great deal of Yeats in that statement, and in his pride in it. By "we" the father means we Yeatses and I John Butler Yeats. The tongue is the poet-son whom he loved and admired (and instructed). The sea cliffs are the tough tongue-tied Cornish Pollexfens. What most moves the son in the eulogy is to be declared the voice of the noble vision, of the world seen as high, deep, and hard, an arena of tragic experience: to be that sternness softened to the point of speech.

In seeking to understand the meaning of nobility in the life and work of Yeats, I shall glance quickly at a good many passages in his poetry and prose, and longer at four major poems: first that which Eliot called "the violent and terrible epistle dedicatory" to his volume of 1914, *Responsibilities*; then the title poem from *The Tower* of 1928; then two of the great *Last Poems* of 1939, "The Municipal Gallery Revisited" and "High Talk."

First the "Introductory Rhymes" of 1914:

> Pardon, old fathers, if you still remain
> Somewhere in ear-shot for the story's end,
> Old Dublin merchant 'free of ten and four'
> Or trading out of Galway into Spain;
> Old country scholar, Robert Emmet's friend,
> A hundred-year-old memory to the poor;
> Merchant and scholar who have left me blood
> That has not passed through any huckster's loin,
> Soldiers that gave, whatever die was cast:
> A Butler or an Armstrong that withstood
> Beside the brackish waters of the Boyne
> James and his Irish when the Dutchman crossed;
> Old merchant skipper that leaped overboard
> After a ragged hat in Biscay Bay.
> You most of all, silent and fierce old man,
> Because the daily spectacle that stirred
> My fancy, and set my boyish lips to say,
> 'Only the wasteful virtues earn the sun';
> Pardon that for a barren passion's sake,
> Although I have come close on forty-nine,
> I have no child, I have nothing but a book,
> Nothing but that to prove your blood and mine.[1]

How much Yeats is there. Periodically, throughout his life, Yeats felt compelled to write what I think of as roll-calling poems, poems of accountancy and summation, in which persons and motives were commanded to stand forth and shape up, to express and to embody the current, and collective, state of his mind and heart. This is such a poem. W. H. Auden has praised Yeats as the poet who brought back to life in English the occasional poem, verses that celebrate notable events. Auden was thinking of poems like "Easter 1916" or "In Memory of Major Robert Gregory," which are also roll-calling poems in my sense.

But these "Introductory Rhymes" are not quite the kind of thing

---

1. Passages from the poetry of William Butler Yeats are reprinted with permission of Macmillan Publishing Company from *The Collected Works of W. B. Yeats,* ed. Richard J. Finneran, copyright 1916, 1918, 1919, 1924, 1928 by Macmillan Publishing Company, renewed 1944, 1946, 1947, 1952, 1956 by Bertha Georgie Yeats; copyright 1940 by Georgie Yeats, renewed 1968 by Bertha Georgie Yeats, Michael Butler Yeats, and Anne Yeats.

Auden had in mind. Here the only occasion is personal and small, the publication of a new volume of poems and the poet's arrival at a certain age. Yet Yeats characteristically chooses to make ceremony of these small events. As he wrote the poem in January 1914, he was forty-eight years old; but he does not say "forty-eight," he says "close on forty-nine." What he is thinking of is "fifty," the half-century, a small-scale *magnus annus*. For a man of Yeats's passionate and committed humanism, every event, because it is life and is human, is potentially symbolic and entitled to celebration. His sense of life was like that of Keats, who spoke of "a life like the Scriptures, figurative," and guessed that Shakespeare "led a life of allegory" upon which his works were a "commentary." That sort of view of experience as allegory rising out of myth and pointing back to it was Yeats's view of his own life, indeed of all life.

Here, calling the roll at close on forty-nine, casting up a balance, Yeats is looking at his life as figurative, a metaphor full of meaning. It scarcely matters, or matters positively, that the event he is celebrating is negative, a nonevent; the thing that is occurring is a nonoccurrence. What he is celebrating is his own failure to create and transmit life: "I have no child, I have nothing but a book." The poem is a public and passionate *apologia pro vita sua*, asking pardon of the ranked shades of his ancestors, "Pardon, old fathers," for his failure as a man and as a Yeats. At the same time the poem is a form of prayer. Characteristically, the gods who are supplicated are secular and familial: "Pardon, old fathers." As a child, Yeats tells us in his *Autobiography*, he had confused one of these household gods, the "silent and fierce old man," his grandfather William Pollexfen, with the great God himself.

What is it in his ancestors that stirs and shames the poet, as nearing fifty he draws up for "the story's end"? It is the vivid habits and powers he means by "the wasteful virtues." Roughly, he is claiming for his paternal line the wasteful virtues of learning, charity, bravery, patriotism; for his maternal line he claims enterprise and daring, habitual passionate vitality. It is a pattern loosely aristocratic, at least one form of nobility. The mercantile blood is not denied but it is sublimated; it "has not passed through any huckster's loin." In his view of them Yeats's mercantile ancestors were not shopkeepers; they would not (in Moll Flanders's idiom) have shown the mark of their hats upon their wigs, or the mark of their apron strings upon their coats. They were shipmen and sailors, merchant-adventurers. William Pollexfen bears the scar of a whaling hook in his hand, hunts down enemies with a horsewhip, and displays in his little back parlor a painted coat of arms. When George Pollexfen rides to the race meeting at Sligo he is accompanied by two postilions in green livery.

The pattern is as well significantly Anglo-Irish, a strain after many generations in the land still not native or assimilated, still a bit alien and *rentier*. To be Anglo-Irish was to inherit a tradition of power and privilege, of landed gentility, of comparative wealth and culture, of Protestantism, of suspicious identification with the most hated of absentee proprietors, England herself. It was also to inherit the glory, though not necessarily the genius, of the most astonishingly brilliant and fertile strain in the history of British letters, the Anglo-Irish line that produced Congreve, Swift, Berkeley, Burke, Goldsmith, Sterne, Shaw, Wilde, Synge, Lady Gregory, Joyce Cary, and all the Yeatses.

The *grand seigneur* side of Yeats lasted all his life and if anything intensified with time. It is the hardest side of him to like, at least for an American taste, which finds something repugnant and stagy in his tendency to love a lord, to admire power and privilege, and to adopt its magisterial manners. The elegance of his own genetic line was running thin by the time it reached his father's generation, and Yeats was perfectly capable of seeing as comedy the eccentricity of the older ones about him—of one grandfather who slept with a hatchet against burglars, of another who walked about jingling his keys so as not to surprise his servants in embarrassing attitudes, of the vain Protestant curate who ripped three pairs of skintight trousers before he could mount one horse: "I had hoped for a curate," his rector said, "but they have sent me a jockey."

Certainly John Butler Yeats's family could have had no illusions of wealth or stability. Their life was shabby and peripatetic, though never dull. J. B. Yeats was an admirable father and a gay and noble companion but a bad provider, and for many years everything anybody earned went perforce into what was called the family "swalley hole." Yeats speaks laconically of the "torn tackle" of his equipment, of inking his socks to hide the holes in his shoes. For years, apparently, he was actually undernourished; by housing and feeding him in summers at Coole, Lady Gregory almost certainly extended his life. In view of these surrounding facts of his life, it is tempting to see Yeats's aristocratic leanings as wish-fulfilling and compensatory. One may be reminded of his own view of Keats in "Ego Dominus Tuus" where *Ille*, who speaks for Yeats, says:

> His art is happy, but who knows his mind?
> I see a schoolboy when I think of him,
> With face and nose pressed to a sweet-shop window,
> For certainly he sank into his grave

> His senses and his heart unsatisfied,
> And made—being poor, ailing and ignorant,
> Shut out from all the luxury of the world,
> The coarse-bred son of a livery-stable keeper—
> Luxuriant song.

But Yeats's aristocracy, in this limited and conventional sense, was real and a thing of blood. As a young man he was poor and ailing and even ignorant; but he could never have been called coarse-bred. Yet all this is only a small and distracting part of what I mean by Yeats's nobility, or of his own definition of nobility. The true nobility visible in the "Introductory Rhymes" is less a matter of wealth or breeding than a matter of spirit, a matter of feeling, a matter of noble passion. The wasteful virtues are deeds and feelings of passion and commitment, hot, unthinking and unselfish, generous. They have to do with blood only in the degree to which old blood is likely to be hot blood. The silent and fierce old man whom as a boy Yeats confused with God, as a man he identified with King Lear and thus with the order of wasteful virtues that informs high tragedy. "Even today," he says in *Reveries*, "when I read *King Lear* his image is always before me and I often wonder if the delight in passionate men in my plays and in my poetry is more than his memory." Looking through the family miniatures collected by his sister Lily, who was the squirrel of the Yeats family, he reflected, "I am delighted with all that joins my life to those who had power in Ireland or with those anywhere that were good servants and poor bargainers." To practice the wasteful virtues the thing most necessary is to possess passion and generosity, to be a good servant and a poor bargainer.

It is clear too that the emotion that ultimately drives this poem, the poet's hopeless and unreconciled love for Maud Gonne, though it is bitterly described as "a barren passion," is of the order of nobility. Yeats's wasteful passion, good service and a poor bargain, summons all the ramified nobility of the poem. Maud was his Phoenix, his Helen, his daughter of the swan, his Pallas Athene, his woman Homer sung. To be so is to be noble, and to feel so of a noble person is to join the line of nobility. Such wasteful virtues earn the sun by kinship to it, being luminous and fiery, sprung from what Yeats would later call the resinous heart.

By the time of "The Tower," Yeats's roll-calling poem of 1926, his life was much altered, grander and more stable, in an Ireland detached from England and dismembered in herself, trying to become a modern state though barely alive after a world war, a revolution, and a civil war. Ten years before he had been confident and secure enough to refuse a knighthood, quietly: "I do not wish anyone to say of me, 'only for a ribbon he left us.'" Yeats in 1926 was a senator of the Irish Free State, an internationally famous man of letters, a Nobel prizewinner who had been told that the Swedish royal family preferred him to any other recipient of the prize because he had the manners of a courtier. His inward elegance had moved outward and confirmed itself in that graceful and imposing presence that marked his deportment until the end of his life. And for the first time he knew something like affluence.

His sisters, influenced by the ideals of archaism and craftsmanship of William Morris, as was the poet who called Morris "my chief of men," had prospered modestly in their Cuala Industries, composed of Lily's fine needlework and embroidery and Lolly's fine printing and illumination. Yeats spoke of the traditional feeling that had quickly attached itself to the little Cuala volumes: "My sister's books are like an old family magazine. A few hundred people buy them all and expect a common theme. Only once did I put a book into the series that was not Irish—Ezra's Noh plays—and I had to write a long introduction to annex Japan to Ireland." Jack Yeats was becoming Ireland's best known modern painter, his work given mass and energy by his sympathy with the open-air life of Ireland, with fist-fighters and horsemen and seamen and the rambling tinkers of the roads. The poet kept finding in his brother's pictures faces he remembered from their boyhood on the Sligo quays fifty years before.

Old John Butler Yeats had come to be known in the family as their Pilgrim Father. He went to New York for a visit in 1908, liked it, and stayed on to try out a new incarnation. He had been called the best talker in Dublin, and he was soon known as the best talker in New York, where the competition was less severe. He kept ramshackle *salon* for a circle of writers and painters at his French boardinghouse on West 29th Street. John Sloan painted him there in "Yeats at Petitpas," sketching and talking away to a little crowd about a dinner table in the back garden, in an attitude that recalls his son's image of him in a late poem, "his beautiful mischievous head thrown back." Ezra Pound recalled seeing "the father of all the Yeatsssssss" about 1910 riding an elephant at Coney Island. The new career of the old portrait painter was little more successful than the old. He wrote and lectured and painted, energetically and happily, but he never quite paid his way. He still suffered from his old incapacity to finish crucial pictures. He worked on a self-portrait at John Quinn's commission for ten years, and left it unfinished when he died, the paint by then a half-inch thick. His many letters to his children were vivid and homely documents, intensely human and intelligent; those to the poet particularly composing a piecemeal aesthetics and philosophy warm, original, and profound. W. B. Yeats was quite aware of his deep debt to his father's mind. Composing a lecture in 1910 he found himself working toward a thought which he recognized as his father's, and he reflected how often that had happened. "It made me realize with some surprise," he wrote, "how fully my philosophy of life has been inherited from you in all but its details and applications." Importuned many times to come home to Ireland, J. B. Yeats temporized and delayed, and finally died in New York in 1922 at the age of eighty-two. The son wrote soon after to Olivia Shakespear, "I find it hard to realize my father's death, he has so long been a mind to me, that mind seems to me still thinking and writing."

Meanwhile, still unwilling to substitute the book for the child, Yeats was seeking a wife and a home, a setting for a wife and child. Maud Gonne still refused him, and he turned to her beautiful young daughter Iseult, who also refused. Yeats then turned to Georgiana Hyde-Lees, a young woman half his age whom he had known for several years. She accepted and married him in 1917, and thenceforward she was his beloved George. It was a happy and fruitful marriage. "My wife is a perfect wife," Yeats wrote to Lady Gregory in December of 1917, "kind, wise, and unselfish. I think you were such another young girl once. She has made my life serene and full of order." In a few years George brought him a daughter, Anne, and a son, Michael. She brought him also, through her mediumship, through the "unknown instructors," those "reed-throated whisperers," the means to that ordering of his thought which became *A Vision*.

The physical house of Yeats had changed over these years in what now seems a pattern, and one purposeful and appropriate. His last close link with Sligo had been cut with the death in 1910 of his beloved uncle George Pollexfen, businessman, horseman, and astrologer. Lily, who had been in attendance, reported that the banshee had cried on the night before he died, and Yeats was comforted. Yeats had left the family home in Bedford Park in London for the apartment in Woburn Buildings which connected by a passage with the rooms of Arthur Symons. At several intervals he shared a cottage in Sussex with the brash young American Ezra Pound, who taught him to fence, and to admire "certain noble plays of Japan," the Noh Plays, as expressions of an exotic aristocracy, models of brevity and astringency and symbolism, of blood-nobility, an art so simply noble that by it Yeats thought he might at last escape all the paraphernalia of the commercial theater, and claims of audience. He wrote to John Quinn, "I had thought to escape the press, and people digesting their dinners, and to write for my friends." Such plays he considered might be played in a drawing room or a barn. Those alternatives, the equality of the drawing room and the barn, suggest what nobility was coming to mean for Yeats. After his marriage there were long intervals at Oxford, where Yeats worked in the Bodleian Library, finding it the finest of all houses for the mind, "the most comfortable and friendly library in the world and I suppose the most beautiful." But George was equally horrified, he reported, by the hats and the minds of the dons' wives. Summer after summer, before the marriage, there had been Lady Gregory's modest great house at Coole Park, in some ways the truest of all Yeats's spiritual homes. For him it was the synthesis of the best of Anglo-Ireland, where the widowed great Lady who had made herself in middle age an artist and folklorist, heiress of a long line of blood and wealth and power, herself at once lonely, grand, and simple, attuned to any company in castle and cottage, presided over assorted spartan feasts of the spirit. His debt to her was incalculable, as he knew, and as he frequently and handsomely acknowledged.

Now, after 1916, there was the tower itself, literal and figurative, which gave the title to the poem and the volume. As always in Yeats's life, fact moved toward myth and symbol, and the tower invests his imagery for his last twenty years in a variety of attitudes, solemn or gay or mocking. Yeats acquired the tower for £35. The property consisted of an acre or so of land in the rolling countryside a few miles from Gort, from Coole Park, and from the sea, with a Norman stone tower and attached cottages, the whole half-ruinous. It is important to form an image of the parts and the whole, for all came together to form the emblem. The place is isolated in the countryside, set in the ell formed by a shallow little river flowing past one side and a narrow country road flowing over a stone bridge on another side. Thus it is of the land, of the water, of the road, and, in its isolated verticality, of the sky. It is deep in Ireland and deep in time, the main structure dating back to feudal times. The immensely thick, gray stone walls, pierced by slit windows, rise to form four stories and a battlement. Each story is a single huge square room, and the narrow winding stair of rough worn stone rises past each story to the roof. Yeats called the tower Thoor Ballylee, and he explained his logic in a letter to Olivia Shakespear: "Thoor is Irish for tower and it will keep people from suspecting us of modern gothic and a deer park. I think the harsh sound of 'Thoor' amends the softness of the rest."

Like the equation of drawing room and barn, that union of harsh and soft is what I want to get at, for it helps to explain the fluent functions of the symbol for Yeats. "My idea is to keep the contrast between the medieval castle and the peasant's cottage," he wrote. His nobility required both forms of life. "We shall live on the road like a country man, our white walled cottage with its border of flowers like any country cottage and then the gaunt castle," he said in a letter to Clement Shorter. To John Quinn he wrote of the tower in a vein of gay self-satire: "I am making a setting for my old age, a place to influence lawless youth, with its severity and antiquity." It occurred to him that had he possessed his tower earlier he might have been able to smooth Joyce's lawless and difficult way.

Yeats took the keenest pleasure in assuring the primitive integrity of the reconstruction and furnishing of the castle and the cottage. Local artisans—carpenters, masons, smiths—were to do all the work, overseen by a local builder named Raftery, an emotional man who wept when things went wrong. Massive handmade tables, chairs, and beds were designed by the local craftsman Scott, whom Yeats usually referred to as a "drunken man of genius." Because building materials could not be had in wartime, Yeats triumphantly bought the wreckage of an old mill, "great beams and three-inch planks, and old paving stones." And finally he composed one of his brutal short lyrics, "To Be Carved on a Stone at Thoor Ballylee," as his own part in the country artisanship.

> I, the poet William Yeats,
> With old mill boards and sea-green slates,
> And smithy work from the Gort forge,
> Restored this tower for my wife George;
> And may these characters remain
> When all is ruin once again.

He had bought the house, as he put it in "Meditations in Time of Civil War," "for an old neighbour's friendship," "and decked and altered it for a girl's love." For this, in its gracefully ponderous way, was also a honeymoon cottage: "Beauty and fool together laid," as he was to put it later. And that conjunction, too, suggests the poles of Yeats's nobility.

It is the conjunction I wish to speak of in the poem "The Tower," the seemingly disjunct series of images and ideas that come in train to the poet's mind as he paces upon the battlements of the tower to "send imagination forth / Under the day's declining beam, and call / Images and memories / From ruin or from ancient trees." First he recalls an elegant Mrs. French, cruelly lofty:

> Beyond that ridge lived Mrs. French, and once
> When every silver candlestick or sconce
> Lit up the dark mahogany and the wine,
> A serving-man, that could divine
> That most respected lady's every wish,
> Ran and with the garden shears
> Clipped an insolent farmer's ears
> And brought them in a little covered dish.

Immediately, without hesitation, the mind moves to a nameless peasant girl, celebrated for her beauty by a blind folk poet, and the men maddened by poetry and wine and love who set out to find her by moonlight: "And one was drowned in the great bog of Cloone." He pauses to reflect on the phenomenon of a blind poet admiring a girl's beauty, but leaps at once to the oneness and inextricableness of human passion:

> Strange, but the man who made the song was blind;
> Yet, now I have considered it, I find
> That nothing strange; the tragedy began
> With Homer that was a blind man,
> And Helen has all living hearts betrayed.

And he recalls that he himself had behaved as oddly as the blind poet Raftery, in creating Hanrahan and sending him off to follow a hare and hounds made from a pack of cards, so that "he stumbled, tumbled, fumbled to and fro / And had but broken knees for hire / And horrible splendour of desire." The mind now swings home to the tower itself, the history or legend of its occupants: "an ancient bankrupt," harried to death, rough men-at-arms who "climbed the narrow stair" "cross-gartered to the knees / Or shod in iron," or certain ghostly men-at-arms who interrupted sleepers with the noise of their great wooden dice.

It is a fantastic roll that Yeats is calling. Those who are summoned form a company in being ancient, local, and passionate, a nobility of fire and commitment, the kind of folk who might be hoped to have an answer to a certain disastrous question about to be asked by the present master of the house:

> As I would question all, come all who can;
> Come old, necessitous, half-mounted man;
> And bring beauty's blind rambling celebrant;
> The red man the juggler sent
> Through God-forsaken meadows; Mrs. French,
> Gifted with so fine an ear;

> The man drowned in a bog's mire,
> When mocking Muses chose the country wench.

What Yeats at past sixty-one wants to know is whether all of them were tortured as he is by the passing of time and the losing of life:

> Did all old men and women, rich and poor,
> Who trod upon these rocks or passed this door,
> Whether in public or in secret rage
> As I do now against old age?

But a noble old man of property ought to make a will, and that is what Yeats does in the long trimeter paragraphs that close out the poem. The property he bequeaths, however, is primarily spiritual, more ideal than real. Having prepared his peace with learning and poetry and love, "all those things whereof / Man makes a superhuman / Mirror-resembling dream," what he has left to bequeath are his pride and his faith. His pride is Irish but superpolitical, brave, free, generous, impassioned:

> The pride of people that were
> Bound neither to Cause nor to State,
> Neither to slaves that were spat on,
> Nor to the tyrants that spat,
> The people of Burke and of Grattan
> That gave, though free to refuse—
> Pride, like that of the morn,
> When the headlong light is loose,
> Or that of the fabulous horn,
> Or that of the sudden shower
> When all streams are dry,
> Or that of the hour
> When the swan must fix his eye
> Upon a fading gleam,
> Float out upon a long
> Last reach of glimmering stream
> And there sing his last song.

His faith is religious but unchristian, an assertion of the power of man's impassioned will to force upon life and death a sufficient shape and significance:

> I mock Plotinus' thought
> And cry in Plato's teeth,
> Death and life were not
> Till man made up the whole,

> Made lock, stock and barrel
> Out of his bitter soul,
> Aye, sun and moon and star, all.
> And further add to that
> That, being dead, we rise,
> Dream and so create
> Translunar Paradise.

And who are Yeats's heirs? Ordinary noble men, young, active, self-defined, lonely integrities:

> upstanding men
> That climb the streams until
> The fountain leap, and at dawn
> Drop their cast at the side
> Of dripping stone.

Like the tower itself, the poem is a ramshackle monolith, casually impregnable, held together, really, by the noble old energy of complex but purified passion.

"The Municipal Gallery Revisited" of Yeats's *Last Poems* is a roll-calling poem of a more specific and consistent kind. The poet must be seen as an old man communing alone with racial shades, "the images of thirty years," the ancestors of modern Ireland. It is the portraits that seize and hold him, significant countenances, dead but speaking. There are the patriots, political men, Casement, Griffith, O'Higgins. There is the face of a nameless woman, "beautiful and gentle in her Venetian way," whom he remembers seeing "all but fifty years ago / For twenty minutes in some studio." Thinking of time and passion and beauty and sacrifice, the old poet is invaded by a sudden unbidden wave of feeling, shaken to the point of tears: "Heart-smitten with emotion I sink down, / My heart recovering with covered eyes." Touching in its privacy and impressive in its susceptibility, that vision surprises Yeats's noble nature in action for us, defined by the capacity to feel and to value noble bearing and noble work to the base of his being.

Yeats's eyes move next to images of the Coole Park line, Lady Gregory, her son Robert Gregory, her nephew Hugh Lane. All are dead in fact but live on in feeling in a way the canvas cannot contain: "But where is the brush that could show anything / Of all that pride and that humility?" Yeats asks. Pride and humility: once again it is the fusion at the center of the nobility he loved, hymned, and embodied. All the Gregorys are gone and even the great house is gone where, as he puts it, "honour had lived so long." But this mechanical passing he cannot mourn.

The life of that house had a quality that lives on superior to the envy of time and of fresher, smaller motives. "No fox can foul the lair the badger swept."

That was, Yeats parenthesizes, "an image out of Spenser and the common tongue." Once more it is the noble conjunction of the elegant, the ancient, the traditional, the common. Now Yeats collects the images of the trinity he wished might have stood together to receive the Nobel Prize—himself, John Synge, Lady Gregory, now forever united in his feeling in the common-noble "dream of the noble and the beggar-man."

> John Synge, I and Augusta Gregory, thought
> All that we did, all that we said or sang
> Must come from contact with the soil, from that
> Contact everything Antaeus-like grew strong.
> We three alone in modern times had brought
> Everything down to that sole test again,
> Dream of the noble and the beggar-man.

Yeats moves finally to Synge's own image, whom he describes only in the packed phrase, "that rooted man." "Think where man's glory most begins and ends," he invites us at the end of the poem, "and say my glory was I had such friends." Man's glory most begins and ends in high passions, rising out of the common life and wishing finally to speak only to that. In the spring of 1937 Yeats commended an essay on his work by Archibald MacLeish as "the only article on the subject which has not bored me for years." MacLeish had praised the diction of his poetry as "public." "That word, which I had not thought of myself, is a word I want," Yeats wrote to Lady Dorothy Wellesley. Thinking earlier of his ideal auditor, his Connemara fisherman, Yeats had cried,

> Before I am old
> I shall have written him one
> Poem maybe as cold
> And passionate as the dawn.

That is why the tower had to rise out of the stream and the earth, and why the cottages had to remain at its base, to tie it Antaeus-like to the soil, to prevent its wish to soar off into the lofty and the abstract.

Two final Irish houses of Yeats require brief mention. Each in its way preserves the unity of the pattern of his habitation. Early in 1922, with the tower still barely habitable only in summer, George Yeats tired fatally of the hats of the dons' wives in Oxford and resolved to find a house in Dublin. "My Saturn suggested delay but her Mars carried it and she went," Yeats wrote to Olivia Shakespear. Again their luck held and Mrs. Yeats found at a bargain a fine tall Georgian house at 82 Merrion Square. With some complacency Yeats explained to Mrs. Shakespear that Merrion Square was to Dublin what Berkeley Square was to London. The house had been built about 1740 with rooms "very large and stately" and handsome mantelpieces. Yeats felt, he wrote, "very grand" remembering a street ballad about the Duke of Wellington: "In Merrion Square / This noble hero first drew breath / Amid a nation's cheers." It was an elegant house, withal plain, an appropriate setting for a man who within the next year was to be a senator of Ireland, a Litt.D. of Trinity College, Dublin, and a holder of the Nobel Prize.

In May of 1932 Lady Gregory died. Yeats wrote, "I have lost one who has been to me for nearly forty years my strength and my conscience." At Coole he heard a ragged Dublin sculptor, who had called to pay his respects, musing, after staring about him at the pictures of the great who had been associated with that house, "All the nobility of earth." "I felt he did not mean it for that room alone but for lost tradition," Yeats wrote. He continued: "How much of my own work has not been but the repetition of those words." In the same summer Yeats occupied his last Irish house, smaller and more simplified like life itself for him. What he called "this little creeper-covered farm-house" was named Riversdale and was situated in Rathfarnham, "just too far from Dublin to go there without good reason and too far, I hope, for most interviewers and the less determined travelling bores." For Edith Shackleton Heald he drew a plan of his study and went on to describe it:

> All round the study walls are book-cases but some stop half way up and over them are pictures by my brother, my father, by Robert Gregory. On each side of the window into [the] flower garden are two great Chinese pictures (Dulac's gift) and in the window into the greenhouse hangs a most lovely Burne-Jones window (Ricketts's gift). Through the glass door into the flower garden I see the bare boughs of apple trees and a few last flowers.

Through french doors he would walk out into the garden to "share the gooseberries with the bullfinches." Outside there was space for fruit trees, croquet and tennis lawns, and a bowling green.

This is an elegant simplicity, but a simplicity, and it was in a real sense a return to the earth, an Antaeus-gesture. Yeats thought of Riversdale as a last place in life. "We have a lease for but thirteen years but that will see me out of life," he wrote to Mrs. Shakespear. Violent poetic work went on in this quiet place, the splendid extravagance of the passion of the final lyrical flowing-out of the poet self-defined as "foolish, passionate man," "a wild old wicked man." We can watch the house itself erupt into grand romantic passion within a single poem, "An Acre of Grass."

> Picture and book remain,
> An acre of green grass
> For air and exercise,
> Now strength of body goes;
> Midnight, an old house
> Where nothing stirs but a mouse.
>
> My temptation is quiet.
> Here at life's end
> Neither loose imagination,
> Nor the mill of the mind
> Consuming its rag and bone,
> Can make the truth known.
>
> Grant me an old man's frenzy,
> Myself must I remake
> Till I am Timon and Lear
> Or that William Blake
> Who beat upon the wall
> Till Truth obeyed his call;
>
> A mind Michael Angelo knew
> That can pierce the clouds,
> Or inspired by frenzy
> Shake the dead in their shrouds;
> Forgotten else by mankind,
> An old man's eagle mind.

"Passion to me is the essential," Yeats had written. In a letter to Wyndham Lewis he made clear what passion meant to him, highly defined; he spoke of "passion ennobled by intensity, by endurance, by wisdom. We had it in one man once. He lies in St. Patrick's now under the greatest epitaph in history." The reference of course is to Jonathan Swift.

One who had followed Yeats's own accumulation of passion ennobled by intensity, by endurance, by wisdom, might barely have hoped for something so magnificent at the end as the "bitter and gay" *Last Poems*. It is now that he forms such creatures as Crazy Jane and Tom the Lunatic and John Kinsella lamenting for his old bawd Mrs. Mary Moore. This is Old Man Yeats content at last to "lie down where all the ladders start, / In the foul rag-and-bone shop of the heart." Looking about him at the anarchic modern landscape where once again there's a light in Troy, the world "turning and turning in the widening gyre," where "things fall apart; the center cannot hold," he reacts in a brilliant saturnine irony, a cackling approving curse, a kind of affirmative for which he finds his own proper phrase, "tragic joy."

> Irrational streams of blood are staining earth;
> Empedocles has thrown all things about;
> Hector is dead and there's a light in Troy;
> We that look on but laugh in tragic joy.

"What matter?" he inquires. "Out of cavern comes a voice, / And all it knows is that one word 'Rejoice!'"

"For laughter too is a passion," as Longinus affirmed long ago. Noble men, in any case, are not going to submit to the death of nobility.

> Those that Rocky Face holds dear
> Lovers of horses and of women, shall
> From marble of a broken sepulchre,
> Or dark betwixt the polecat and the owl,
> Or any rich, dark nothing disinter
> The workman, noble and saint, and all things run
> On that unfashionable gyre again.

What he is involved in, the old poet sees, is simply life, the recurrent native forms of experience, a time of the time of man. It has all happened before and will happen again, with tears and laughter.

> On their own feet they came, or on shipboard,
> Camel-back, horse-back, ass-back, mule-back,
> Old civilisations put to the sword.
> Then they and their wisdom went to rack:
> No handiwork of Callimachus,
> Who handled marble as if it were bronze,
> Made draperies that seemed to rise
> When sea-wind swept the corner, stands;
> His long lamp-chimney shaped like the stem
> Of a slender palm, stood but a day;
> All things fall and are built again
> And those that build them again are gay.

Perhaps the strangest, truest, most exhilarating shape Yeats found to embody his last nobility is the stilt-walking hero of "High Talk." He is a lofty clown figure, both artist and artisan, both man and myth, both father and child. He is an extravagant attenuation, teetering, grimacing, just dangerously controlled on the edge of unreason, a funny and terrible fusion of Yeats's central conjunctions: workman and noble and saint, hunchback and saint and fool. He is all metaphor, Malachi, stilts and all. Earlier Yeats had spoken of art as "but a vision of reality"; now, even in the prose of his letters, he is using such phrases as "the madness of vision." Here is the whole poem, which is among other things a travesty of a Petrarchan sonnet, in octave and sestet, but rhymed in couplets, and cast in long snaky hexameters of dactyl and anapest:

> Processions that lack high stilts have nothing that catches the eye.
> What if my great-granddad had a pair that were twenty foot high.
> And mine were but fifteen foot, no modern stalks upon higher,
> Some rogue of the world stole them to patch up a fence or a fire.
> Because piebald ponies, led bears, caged lions, make but poor shows,
> Because children demand Daddy-long-legs upon his timber toes,
> Because women in the upper storeys demand a face at the pane,
> That patching old heels they may shriek, I take to chisel and plane.
>
> Malachi Stilt-Jack am I, whatever I learned has run wild,
> From collar to collar, from stilt to stilt, from father to child.
> All metaphor, Malachi, stilts and all. A barnacle goose
> Far up in the stretches of night; night splits and the dawn breaks loose;
> I, through the terrible novelty of light, stalk on, stalk on;
> Those great sea-horses bare their teeth and laugh at the dawn.

The speaker of those lines has news for the Delphic Oracle. His is a vision that sees so much, so far, so wide, so high, and so deep that it must be mad. It rises out of the vision of life as tragedy but expresses itself as satyr-comedy. Those eyes, those ancient glittering eyes, are gay. I suggest that the poem lays out, with splendid angularity, the limits and the main members of the nobility of the house of Yeats. It is traditional and familial, it has run wild from father to child, it inherits (almost) the heroic height of a twenty-foot great-granddad. It makes its own vestment by its own craft applying its own tools to its own cheap native materials: it takes to chisel and plane. It stretches the human figure presumptuously, grandly, and comically toward the sky without ever losing touch of the earth: Daddy-long-legs upon his timber toes. It is sophisticated and innocent. Its function is to make shows, processions, to leer upon children and men and women at their ordinary work with astonishing grimaces from surprising heights. And then to stalk on through the terrible novelty of light to the place where night splits and the dawn breaks loose.

In the postscript of a letter to Ethel Mannin a few months before he died, Yeats wrote of the arrangements he was making for his burial. "It will be in a little remote country churchyard in Sligo, where my great grandfather was the clergyman a hundred years ago." He quoted the now famous lines from "Under Ben Bulben" which he designed for his epitaph: "Cast a cold eye / On life, on death; / Horseman, pass by." Typically, at the end, Yeats wished to lie down where all his ladders started. When he spoke of his plans to his sister Lily she commented dryly, "This is a break with tradition. There has not been a tombstone in the Yeats family since the eighteenth century. The family has always been very gay." The Yeats habit, he explained to Edith Shackleton Heald, was to "let the grass grow over the dead and speak of them no more." The tombstone would be a ceremonious addition, but in Sligo churchyard Yeats would still be robed in the long friends.

Among those stilt-walkers who are poets, no modern stalks upon higher ground than Yeats. And not many ancients. What he shares with the other greatest poets is uniqueness. In the long run he is only himself, self-defined—self-born, after all. He mocks our enterprise, though we must do our best to praise him.

Putting in the Self
V. S. Pritchett

In thinking about the autobiographical writings of the Irishman Frank O'Connor, I got interested in traits and tendencies of the man that seemed to be not only individual but national or racial, and it occurred to me that one might learn something by studying him alongside his English contemporary V. S. Pritchett, whose case offered striking if accidental parallels. Both were guttersnipes who turned out to be inspired. Pritchett was born over a toy shop in Ipswich in 1900; three years later O'Connor was born over a sweet-and-tobacco shop in Cork City. Each survived poverty, a tortured home situation, and a makeshift education, and rose by talent and force of will to gentility, a high personal civilization, and a distinguished literary career. Each wrote two volumes of reminiscence, the first covering childhood and adolescence, the second carrying the story into full manhood and the solid beginning of professional life. But whereas O'Connor left his second volume unperfected when he was cut off by death in 1966, Pritchett is still with us; and one hopes he may be tempted to go on to a third volume, even though the second, *Midnight Oil*, closes with an air of finality. When I tried to write about the two men together, I found it impossible to accommodate the necessary matter in an essay of tolerable length, and I was forced to divide the study into two papers with cross-references that I hope will be useful.

Pritchett describes his origins as lower middle class; but it is more helpful to think of his people, like O'Connor's, as perilously citified peasants. His mother was an authentic cockney shop-girl, though only one generation from Bedfordshire. "I raised you from the gutter," her husband liked to shout at her—though the family's elevation never reached higher than the curb and they were forever tumbling down again. Victor, the oldest of four children, recalls his mother as a passionate disorderly creature, "lively, sexy and sharp-spoken"; she was "changeable, moody, and in the long run, not to be trusted," with a habit of leaving her sentences suspended at the point of most acute salacious suggestiveness.

107

"This cock-sparrow, my father," Walter, or, in his palmy days, Sawdon Pritchett, an extraordinary Micawber of a man, drives the family through its hectic courses. Bold, strutting, and egotistical, he was a dandified, fastidious little man who in middle age grew enormously fat. Yet there was something curiously impersonal about his self-indulgence, a program merely systematic or official. When he feeds or dresses or lodges in a grand manner he sees himself as embodying his family; and they honor this view of things: the children wait to open the door for him on his return and his wife unbuttons his boots. His business history is a chronicle of petty disasters, yet he never doubts his own destiny or worries because it is to be arranged at the cost of others. V. S. Pritchett's first volume, *A Cab at the Door*, takes its title from the family's habit of moving lodgings after each new failed enterprise: "A cabby and his horse would be coughing together outside the house and the next thing we knew we were driving to an underground station and to a new house in a new part of London, to the smell of new paint, new mice dirts, new cupboards." When Victor is twelve his mother counts fourteen removals; when Walter Pritchett shows offense at her figure, she counts again and now reckons it at eighteen. Walter Pritchett is brash and rash, a fop and a fool, yet an improbably formidable man, impregnable in his self-esteem, keeping his wife and children awed and exasperated as long as he lives.

One of the resources of his tyranny is his piety, which he inherits in turn from his own father, a son of Hull fisher-folk who had made himself into a Congregational minister after years as a soldier and a bricklayer. Married to a hectoring house-proud woman mad on cleanliness, Grandfather Pritchett lived out his life as pastor of a succession of smaller and smaller Yorkshire village chapels. From his parents Walter Pritchett takes the obsessive religiosity that carries him into one tin-roof sect after another until he comes to rest in the Divine Mind of Mary Baker Eddy. Like everything else about him, his piety is factitious but impermeable, an absurdity that he makes a reality by respecting it absolutely because it is his; and it all goes to thicken his pompous, false, and adamantine crust.

Especially in the early years of most painful hardship, young Victor is farmed out for long periods to his grandparents; and in the Yorkshire villages and moors he divines a steadiness, a spaciousness, a natural life of the body, and a hard peasant adequacy to the event that he had never met in his shifting London experience. From the moors he takes a permanent tendency of his thinking and writing: a mystique of place, a sort of secular transcendentalism that sees design and significant content in landscape. And elements of Yorkshire "character" become traits of his own forming nature: a tendency to "truculence and insubordination" running indeed through the whole family, "a strain of gritty, North Country contempt and sarcasm in all of us." It amounts to a defensive aggressiveness, a necessary obduracy, a way of coping with a hard world. It gave Pritchett a certain hardness of finish that Frank O'Connor, for example, never acquired. O'Connor remained always a more vulnerable man.

Still Pritchett's personality, like his parents' marriage, was a union of North and South; and it was undoubtedly his London life that was decisive—though in a sense what that taught him were cockney forms of the same qualities: irreverence, ironical gaiety, energy, inventiveness, a tough capacity for making do. It was London that equipped the boy to say, when his genteel cousin Hilda tried to correct his manners: "I'll kick you up the arse hole. I'll bung up your lug." It was London—cockney realism, I suppose—that equipped the mature man to recall the episode, with chagrin but without shame, as a representative datum.

The Pritchett union was also "like a marriage of the rich and the poor," with Walter Pritchett carrying himself like a grandee as he races his creditors while his wife lives like an unpaid charwoman. He is effortlessly faithful to her because, as his son divines, fundamentally he hates women and can tolerate them only as menials. There is a period during which the children hear their mother denouncing "that woman" through closed doors, but the rival turns out to be only Mary Baker Eddy, in whose Boston yogibogeybox Walter had at last found a spiritual home. At about the same time Sawdon Pritchett, as he now called himself, made his first and only modest success in business in an art needlework manufactory in Newgate Street, catering to the Edwardian lust for draping the person and the premises.

The rootlessness of the Pritchetts' London life, coupled with a native hostility to rote learning, made a shambles of Victor's formal education. He passes through a series of third-rate elementary schools, learning nothing well except Pitman's shorthand—to which he interestingly traces his lasting affection and aptitude for foreign languages. Like O'Connor, though less intensely because less privately, he also passes through the elegant dream school-world of the boys' weeklies, the *Gem* and the *Magnet*, where indolent youths "'strolled' round 'the Quad' and rich uncles tipped them a 'fivah' which they spent on more food." Whereas in the family there has grown up a mysterious legend as to his genius, very little of the testable kind of knowledge has stuck to him. When he sits for the examination that will determine whether he may go on to preparatory school and the university he is sick with fright and diarrhea but upheld by faith in his genius. The examination turned out to be less interested in his genius than in fact, and when he answered questions with fanciful narratives ending in formal laments, his genius did not win a scholarship. He would have to make his own education and his own life.

Within these apparently wasted years two important things have occurred. In Rosendale Road School in Dulwich, W. W. Bartlett has come forward to occupy the office that Daniel Corkery filled for the boy Frank O'Connor, offering the kind of teaching that by precept and example makes learning seem an admirable thing. And under Bartlett's influence young Pritchett makes a beginning at serious if unsystematic reading. By the age of twelve or so he has determined that he is to be a writer and that his metier is to be prose. Already he dimly understands that poetry is an affair too inward and equivocal for his temperament; prose seems to work amid "the common experiences and the solid worlds where judgments were made and in which one could firmly tread." His instincts are moral and pragmatical.

When he is not yet sixteen the lad is abruptly removed from school and sent to work as an office boy in "the leather trade" at a large factor's in Bermondsey. Here he remained for four years. It is characteristic of Pritchett's sane realism not to treat the long interval as a waste or to recall it with condescension or self-pity. For him the leather trade—the craft itself, the people in it, its human and commercial ganglia in the city—is full of energy and instruction, a rich mine of the kind of life that he sees as the province of prose. In the leather factor's warehouse "story after story" walks in. He learns a respect for a craftsman's skill, for traditional expertness, that will stay with him all his life. Pritchett saves his lunch money to buy books, and spends most of his free time exploring the city that fascinates him, walking miles in all directions from his center south of the river.

At the same time he begins attending university-extension lectures, and writes an assigned essay on Milton: "I do not remember what I said in that paper, but I do know that I had started to be interested in unusual words, in the search for the *mot juste*—as it was then called. I chose words for what I called their intensity. I wanted to be terse and exact. I wanted each word to burn into the page. My pen tortured the paper." He experiences the exquisite pleasure of hearing the lecturer speak of his paper as "in a class by itself, . . . obviously by a professional writer"; for the nameless, half-literate boy, a first authentic triumph.

Pritchett is very frank and funny about adolescent sexuality, which torments him unbearably throughout these years. His "organ," he finds, is constantly standing up of its own will. He is mystified and frightened and fiercely attracted by women, and he watches the blatant office intrigues with hot envious eyes. On an errand to his employer's office he is so affected by a view of the secretary's breasts inside her blouse that his head reels and he has to hold onto the desk to save himself from fainting. The girl smiles at him in knowing sympathy.

The men about him do have a few other things on their minds, and it is Hobbs, the most expert of the office sensualists, who sets him to reading the English journalists of the day: W. J. Locke, DuMaurier, Belloc, Wells, Barrie, Stevenson. Pritchett feels a quick affinity for these writers of the second rank. A passage in J. M. Barrie's novel about journalists teaches him "instantly" how to write a short sketch. He thinks of these men as the "travellers," men who move about the world, preferably on foot or with a donkey, and come back to tell of their souls' experience. From them he hears an insistent "whisper" urging him to go abroad, to break free.

It is a long serious illness in the postwar influenza epidemic that finally separates him from the leather trade and frees him to leave England and his family. His fortune consists of twenty pounds—enough, his father estimates, to keep him in Paris for a month. The young man's sensations are not nearly so grand as Stephen Dedalus's hawklike man flying sunward above the sea: he feels frightened, exhilarated, and stubborn, quietly resolved never to return. On the channel steamer his foot is trodden upon by a big blond man who turns out to be Georges Carpentier, the French heavyweight champion. On the train to Paris he tastes wine for the first time and finds it vinegary; but he is "committed" to liking it. The little transitional experiences are to be taken as premonitory.

So ends *A Cab at the Door,* about which one's feelings have been locally powerful but confused in sum, suspended. It is an effect, one supposes, of Pritchett's own feelings about the quality of his life in childhood and youth. The dominant impression is that of a hectic busyness, humming, hivelike, without clear direction or clear lines of emphasis: evidently the life was like that. The book like the boy is dominated by the family, and the family is dominated by the schizoid father, a small man driven by a need to be big: vain, unrealistic, tyrannical, totally undependable. The cab appears at the door too many times. It is a life without order or delicacy, in a family where, as Pritchett put the case in his second volume, "manners were unknown, where everyone shouted, and no one had any notion of taste, either good or bad. We lived without it." Yet the life has style of its own peculiar kind: the hive, especially young Victor, buzzes with energy and talent that seeks a vent and a way to work. The hive of the family is set inside the larger hive of lower-middle-class London, likewise elbowing, raucous, deprived, making do. One watches Victor defining his own nature and painfully, with heaves and lurches, pulling it free.

Pritchett writes of these matters in a style that is admirable for the level of feeling he means to allow expression. His mode is direct, clear, energetic, undecorated, dry: a sharpshooter's or perhaps a sniper's language. The vision at work is attentive and retentive, deprecatory—especially of the self, amused but sardonic, not particularly forgiving. What it sees is a comedy but not a jolly one, an ironical comedy that encloses a lot of suffering—yet the suffering is underplayed, by no means exploited. The language, the vision, one is tempted to call heartless, but that would be both uncharitable and inaccurate. Pritchett's manner is not heartless, but it is remarkably cool: call it emotionally underspecified.

The thing that is missing in the narrative is important: love. The word, or even the idea, is rarely mentioned in *A Cab at the Door*, and almost never in association with the family or any member of it. Like taste, love appears to be a thing the Pritchetts "lived without." It is only in middle life, and then with the help of another's insight, that Pritchett comes at last to see, for example, that his absurd vainglorious father had been a man tortured with affection and anxiety for his children. No doubt it is partly English reticence in personal narrative that makes Pritchett so wary of emotional commitment in his autobiography. But the matter seems more personal and peculiar than that; and one feels that the tendency is not only an effect of style but a fact of life, something in the man.

By ordinary literary-critical standards Pritchett's second volume, *Midnight Oil*, is a denser, finer, more "valuable" book than his first. Its essential subject is vocation: V. S. Pritchett making a beginning as a writer, finding direction by a mixture of purpose, accident, and necessity, reaching an established position. In all senses it is a professional book. It is full of matter and of wisdom. Within its set limits, it is actually more open, freer, warmer in expressed emotion than *A Cab at the Door*. Especially in its unpretentious way of presenting the self and its wise and straight way of talking about the craft of writing, it is a very winning book and an instructive one. Yet in turning professional Pritchett has become curiously less interesting. Perversely one finds oneself missing the very thing that had got on one's nerves in the first volume: the remorseless herky-jerky tension of the domestic comedy-drama. Pritchett by himself, turning literary, finding success, is a less involving figure than Pritchett beating his wings frantically in the hive of the family. The second book lacks the hectic vitality of the first, and the gain in serenity does not altogether compensate.

Once again the span is about twenty years, by no means evenly distributed. The first seven years, which include crucial periods in France, Ireland, and Spain, are treated in fullest detail, and indeed the first two years, in Paris, fill well over a third of the book. For Pritchett these seven years compose "the period when a writer has not yet become one, or just having become one, is struggling to form his talent." Of course for a young man who must make his way entirely on his own, the period is also a sometimes desperate struggle for simple survival.

Midnight Oil begins in a touching, gravely humorous way, with V. S. Pritchett at seventy years contemplating two photographs of himself. One is contemporary and shows a bald aging man writing on a pastry board: "His fattish face is supported by a valance of chins; the head is held together by glasses that slip down a bridgeless nose"; the other shows the same man as a youth of twenty sitting on a table in Paris: he looks vague, shapeless, cocky, histrionic. Pritchett says it is the "embarrassment" he feels at that early image that forms the subject of his book. He is trying to make peace with that image, and to make sense of it: to understand, so to speak, how he got from there to here. He writes, as he puts the matter movingly, out of the general mystification of age and experience: "One is less and less sure of who one is"; and from the point of view of the cumulative anonymity, the evacuated persona of the artist: "The professional writer who spends his time becoming other people and places, real or imaginary, finds he has written his life away and has become almost nothing."

It would be too much to call the two years in Paris decisive: they were the exhausting instructive crucial first phase of a definition. Paris, being "built for Art and Learning," seemed "made for" Pritchett; the London he already knew so well had been "built for government and trade." His first "intoxication" was the pleasure of being purely alone for the first time in his life: to know nobody, to be himself to make. There is nothing grand or accomplished about Pritchett's early acquaintance with Parisian art and learning. It is a patchy, spasmodic bootstrap operation in which he snatches what he can in his small free time. He still has to labor to survive at all. His education is still a thing he "picks up" as he goes along, as he "needs it." He is still in the grip of his "vulgar" notion of literature as an arcane corpus, ever growing, after which he must run panting to "catch up"—to reach it, to come abreast. It is wholly unconsciously that Pritchett inhabits the Paris of the great expatriate generation: he does not share it, he doesn't know that it exists. He has never heard of the Steins, of James Joyce or Ezra Pound or Sylvia Beach, of Hemingway or Scott Fitzgerald.

Pritchett finds a first job as an assistant in a photographer's shop, and a decent cheap room in Auteuil in the flat of a youngish war widow who comes into his room on Sundays when he is stripped for a general wash, and stands talking about her life: nothing particularly sexy about it—just companionable. He "eats his way through the cheap streets of Paris." Soon he is fluent in two kinds of French, polite and less polite. As in London he walks a great deal, and he often sits over a glass of coffee or beer for hours in an evening, absorbing the vigor and variousness of Parisian life. On fine weekends he takes to the open road, walking as far as Chartres for example, coming back covered with dust and with a full notebook. He takes a plunge: following Barrie's advice "to write on the smallest things and those near to you," he writes and rewrites three little sketches and sends them off to English reviews and the *Christian Science Monitor*, the journal of the family sect. All three are accepted and Pritchett "hummed inside with the giddiness of my genius." He is "a writer." But when he rereads one of the pieces a bit later he finds it disgusts him. He feels his first attack of the lifelong terror that accompanies the writer's act of impersonation: "the depression and sense of nothingness that comes when a piece of work is done. The satisfaction is in the act itself; when it is over there is relief, but the satisfaction is gone. After fifty years I still find this to be so, and that with every new piece of writing I have to make that terrifying break with my real life and learn to write again, from the beginning."

Of course he can only persist, and in the whole program: working, learning, writing. He falls into a new job as a salesman in "the shellac trade." He is a failure, but the fact takes time to emerge, and in the meanwhile he is earning twice as much and he is enchanted to be exploring Balzac's bourgeois Paris as he shows his samples of shellac and glue and copal gum. There are the usual phantasmagoric episodes. Pritchett and another salesman are ordered to spend a week under a broiling summer sun shoveling tons of adulterated copal through sieves; one night as they are sluicing the dust off themselves under a pump they are attacked by a crowd of jeering factory girls who pull down their trousers:

"Look at his little toy," shouts one of the girls. His self-willed toy is still a terrible problem, and he is tortured by desire and consoled only by fantasies. For weeks he is involved in a somnambular affair, platonic and impassioned, with the fey Judy, the young daughter of an Edwardian adventuress who finally departs with the girl and ten pounds of Pritchett's scanty cash.

Blushing and stammering, he buys in a druggist's shop what he believes is a package of contraceptives, as a hedge against a hopeful future. Finally he is taken sweetly to bed for the first time in his life by Hester, a tall Danish girl who is in Paris to write a dissertation on the philosopher Malebranche. When he reaches for his contraceptives he discovers that what he has been sold is a package of liver pills. He gulps down two of the pills anyway: perhaps the French know of a relationship between the liver and the sexual machinery. Matters proceed, and after the event the young people go out and walk "tenderly by the river, where the lights were going down like spears into the water." When Hester comprehends the story of the liver pills she is so helpless with shouting laughter that he has to hold her up.

Pritchett has heard of postcoital disgust and guilt, but he feels nothing of the kind now, and indeed he never will. Sex remains for him simply a great gift of the creator to the creature, one of the things that make it possible to live. What he feels now is the small triumph, the pleasure of unprecedented intimacy, and the comic coloring of his own performance. Throughout the Paris interval Pritchett's view of his life continues comic: "What I am really remembering is the uncouth figure I cut." There is little chagrin in his retrospection. His control is an expression of an engaging candor and sanity that allow him to see his history not only as personal, the history of an ego, a vanity, but as representative data in a standard human demonstration. The comedy of *Midnight Oil* extends and matures that of *A Cab at the Door:* it is gayer, more affirmative, less embarrassed and wounded.

By the time Pritchett is sacked from his job in the shellac trade he has acquired enough confidence to think of making a living by writing. The editor of the *Monitor* makes an appearance in Paris, and he says, "I like your stuff. I'll take ten more." But now, with a market assured, the stuff begins to come hard. Pritchett is bored with the sketchy journalistic impressions that he is writing. He feels he has no real subject matter and probably no talent. Furthermore there has been a quarrel in Boston, the Rome of Christian Science; funds are tied up; and he is not being paid for his articles. His cash dwindles, disappears; he is hungry. He begins "eating" his clothes, his typewriter, his books one by one. He is starving. For six days he survives on half a roll a day, then there is nothing. He walks about the streets giddy with emptiness. His landlady fills him up with soup at last, then a stronger miracle occurs: fifteen pounds from a local Scientist embarrassed because Pritchett has not been paid for his work.

He feels he cannot go on any longer living so "thoughtlessly"; he must return at least briefly to England and look for a way to put his life on a steadier footing. As the Paris period draws to a close Pritchett sums up the permanent legacy: he has mastered a second language and done a great deal of reading; he has "rebelled successfully," tried freedom and survived it; without anxiety or remorse he has acquired the courage to be feckless and absurd. He does not feel any achieved identity, however, and he is afraid that he may yet be forced back into the old undiscriminating and constraining mold from which he had wrenched himself two years earlier. But he is a far older, tougher person now, this young man just past his majority.

On the way home he is depressed by the "pink, masked faces" of his "humbugging countrymen." He pauses in London long enough to receive his father's reprimands and his mother's disorderly affection, and to meet the *Monitor*'s avuncular London editor, who pays him his arrears and proposes a new scheme: twenty-five pounds for six articles on the troubles in Ireland, and a possible chance to remain in Ireland for a year as the paper's correspondent. Pritchett accepts at once, as he must, though he knows almost nothing of the country or of the murderous civil war between Free Staters and Republicans that followed the treaty of 1921 with England. He is stumbling into the same crisis that put an end to Frank O'Connor's boyhood.

Arriving in Dublin, he inhales the characteristic odor of horse manure and stout. As he walks about the city he is stopped and searched several times by Free State patrols; after a bit he discovers that his cherished wide-brimmed green velour hat from the Boulevard des Italiens resembles that affected by the IRA. In spite of vivid moments Pritchett's pages on Ireland are the least sharp in images, the least penetrating in analysis of his various views of cultures. Perhaps the softness of the narcotic Irish air has something to do with it, along with the formlessness and pastiche he senses in Irish life arising out of a national displacement in time. "Unknown to myself," Pritchett says at the outset, "I was headed for the seventeenth century." Paying a ritual call at the Abbey Theatre on his first evening, he sees in the foyer a small middle-aged woman "like a cottage loaf" talking with a tall man, very thin: "The woman's voice was quiet and decided. His fell from his height as waveringly as a snowflake." Lady Gregory and Lennox Robinson, of course. Pritchett watches the company going through *The Countess Cathleen* "in sorrowing voices" before an almost empty house: a penalty of civil war.

Pritchett is now officially a "traveller" like his early idols, and so, exploring the country and following the course of the hostilities, he makes a first swing to the south and west, to Cork, Kerry, Tipperary, Limerick, Enniskillen. He sees few of the belligerents, but his route is punctuated by the sound of volleys from machine guns or the rifles of "the boys from the hills." Pritchett finds himself in a sort of daze, overwhelmed by the beauty of the country and the sadness of its emptiness, and bemused by the elusiveness of Irish personality, its slippery bifurcations: "the elaborately disguised curiosity of the impulsively kind but guarded people, looking into your eyes for a chance of capping your fantasy with one of theirs, in long ceremonies of well-mannered evasion, craving for the guesswork of acquaintance and diversion," a longing for relationship coupled with a craving for the back to be turned "to give a bit of malice a chance." Nobody has put the Irish mystery better. Pritchett feels "occupied" by the power of sensation from without: "every movement of light, every turn of leaf, every person"; and emptied of intelligence and will, "thick in the head." In despair of identifying a subject, he is finally driven to "write flatly everything I saw and heard."

To his surprise these first articles are a success and the long-lapsed Scientist is named Irish correspondent of the *Monitor*. The assignment fills a year. Pritchett presents the period in highlights, singly vivid but forming no real shape or cumulative significance. Outside the "Victorian lagoon" of Dublin, he is seeing the Anglo-Irish squirearchy, Somerville and Ross types: a landowner who travels with a system of planks strapped to his car for crossing the ditches "the clowns" keep digging across his roads; a "mad feller," a country banker so traumatized by a severe beating at the hands of Irregulars in a raid on his bank that he is convinced that he "stinks": he slinks away across the fields if he sees anyone coming and finally he takes his own life. In Dublin we get only snapshots: the abysmal slums; Sean O'Casey in his tenement room where he has lettered on the wall GET ON WITH THE BLOODY PLAY; "the beautiful" George Yeats riding a bicycle past St. Stephen's Green; Æ also on a bicycle carrying a bunch of flowers; Æ "drowning" Pritchett in a tide of beautiful mystical phrase-making in his office papered with his own "golden murals of ethereal beings." We pay the obligatory call upon

W. B. Yeats and meet a dandy in delicate tweed who seems only the more remote as he draws nearer, and who empties his pot of used lapsang tea leaves "with a swoosh" out the window into Merrion Square.

None of this cuts very deep, and it is most unsatisfactory as compared to what Frank O'Connor made of the same material; but O'Connor was not a "traveller" in Ireland but an inmate breathing the breath of life. We do learn things from Pritchett: the way the blighting Calvinism lurks just under the Irish surface; the way jokes "ripple" over the skin covering "the incurable seventeenth century bitterness." Yet whereas he realizes that "one has to make something of the way they turn tragedy to farce and farce back into tragedy," it is really an obligation that he ignores. He never pulls the experience together into a meaning, and what one feels finally is that it did not mean enough to him. One comes to wonder if Pritchett's failing first marriage has something to do with the scatty and perfunctory quality of his Irish reminiscences. He marries the young woman, a fellow journalist, more or less on impulse, a mistaken impulse as he presents the case, brought on by the *Monitor*'s recalling him from Ireland and sending him off to Spain with the opulence of £400 a year. This must be the vaguest marriage on public record. Pritchett says almost nothing about the young woman or their relationship, and seems to prefer to treat the whole matter as a thing best forgotten. Does the Irish year suffer unconsciously from that veiling motive? The fact remains that Ireland seems to have meant almost nothing to Pritchett intellectually, and not much more emotionally.

Spain is another matter altogether, for there one can watch V. S. Pritchett come of age, emotionally and intellectually. The shock that he receives from the country and the people is powerful and profound: at once sharp and mysterious, atmospheric and subterranean. One is tempted to call it chthonic: it seems to rise out of the Spanish earth and then to move through the temperament of the people. Pritchett is shaken and changed by both. His imagination had always been topographical: for him as for certain painters landscape had always been nearly a sufficiency in itself, a speaking thing, perhaps oracular. He added people only late and reluctantly, when forced from outside. Pritchett describes the landscape of Castile as he experienced it on his first train journey: "the monotonous yet bizarre moon landscape of flat-topped mesas that proceeded like a geometry under a clear cold sky and dry winter sun." He feels "magnetized" by the sight, and he has a sensation of being looked at rather than looking. The Castilian landscape, where "one could see the bare flesh and bone of the earth," seems a system of absolutes, full of powerful silent purpose:

> Distance was hard and taciturn. The colors themselves were harsher in the foreground and there was, above all, an exact sight of shape and line. The earth did not fade into the transcendental; rock was rock, trees were trees, mountains were mountains and wilderness was wilderness. There was nothing of the "deeply interfused"; there was something that could be known and which it was necessary to know. There was a sense of the immediate and finite, so much more satisfying than the infinite, which had really starved me.

Pritchett insists upon calling the experience the reverse of transcendental. He feels that he is coming awake for the first time in his life, moving out of fantasy into reality: "The transcendentalist dream in which I had lived till then came to an end." He does not see how essentially Emersonian his vision remains. His epiphany is secular in content, and that makes a fundamental difference. The scene for him expresses "the physical not the spiritual." The hardness and clarity of the scene speak to him of the real, an apprehensible essence of a knowable world. Yet its effect upon him must ultimately be called spiritual, in a sense that Emerson would not find alien: "I felt that I was human," Pritchett says simply, radically. Of course the revelation is also aesthetic: "Here one began to see exactly." Pritchett has found his governing principle as a writer: precision, clarity, economy—to get at "the essence" of a thing. He connected it as a style with "the laconic." He had to go to Spain to arrive at the heart of English genius, rooted in the classical, of which he then knew nothing.

Spain takes possession of Pritchett. Many days he spends huddled over a little oil stove reading Spanish history and literature with a concentration entirely new to him. He travels the country restlessly on foot or by train, seeking out essences. But he is growing tired of his life as a correspondent. He "despises" news and is "confused" by opinion; essence must lie elsewhere. He spends weeks writing his first short story, trying at last to make people talk to one another. The *Monitor* sends him off to America. He goes reluctantly and the experience amounts to little of his recollection, the high point being a walking tour in the southern Appalachians where he filled notebooks with the rambling mindless monologues of the poor whites. A second tour in Ireland produces little aside from four short stories, written with great difficulty. His journalistic prose of the period Pritchett later found shaming—tortuously overwritten, far from laconic: "those bizarre lyrical outbursts, those classy metaphors and finicking adjectives." He was trying to compensate for the unconfessed triviality of his subjects by straining for "style." He consoles himself slightly with the reflection that after all youth is "the time of the sincerely insincere," but he was writing so badly, baffling and tiring his readers, that the *Monitor* was right, Pritchett acknowledges, to fire him at last. It turned out to be one of those disasters that for a writer become a liberation.

So he still had himself to make, his metier still to discover. He was only in his middle twenties, and his *wanderjahre*, nearly seven of them with concentrated experience of four countries, had provided him with an extraordinarily rich seed-ground. The remaining third of *Midnight Oil* deals with Pritchett's difficult establishment as an English writer, his ascent to a higher and more varied kind of journalism. The interval is disorderly and decisive. Of course he has to rediscover London, or to discover it for the first time as a literary world. He has little money, no job, no prospects. He knows hardly anyone: even the names of the evidently famous that he begins to hear about are strange to him. When Edward O'Brien advises him to live in Bloomsbury and get to know its famous group, Pritchett has never heard of either the place or the group. When he looks at a map of London he is surprised to find that in his lodging in Tottenham Court Road he has been living on the edge of Bloomsbury for some time.

Pritchett is a prickly young man, as he admits, "too proud" to attach himself to distinguished older men, and in a stubborn class reaction refusing to get on with university-educated men with their "standard precocity"; he is temperamentally hostile to "that sociable, ironic discouragement on which they had been brought up and on which English intellectual society had tested its wits for generations." In fact he was as ironical as they, but less sociable and less discouraged: earthier, more pragmatical and energetic. In Pritchett's kind of struggling history, cultivated weariness was an unaffordable luxury. He did not expect much but he was far from resigned; he did not stop demanding a great deal from life. Pritchett was always to be something of a loner, never a coterie man.

Now he moves about London from one poor furnished room to another, picking up a shilling wherever he can find it. For a time, blessing the wordiness of English, he translates French and Spanish business letters at four words for a penny. He places a few short sketches in the *Manchester Guardian* and the *Outlook*. Sixty pounds received from the sale of his old car in Dublin he divides with his wife, and with capital in hand he decides that a travel book is the thing that he must do. He has been reading Lawrence's *Sea and Sardinia* with "despairing admiration," his despair founded on the question "Why was he so 'inside' his subject and I so brittle, cool and 'outside'?" He tramps across Spain from south to north:

> The weather was good. The sun burned. The nights were cold. I was strong. I did my twenty miles a day, slept in simple *ventas* on the stone floor—after I had sat round a stick fire with the family and ate what the women fried there. The poor were more interesting than the well-off, and the Spanish poor did not whine. They were whole in their manliness and womanliness. I once shared a pigsty with very clean piglets.

In writing his first book he takes a lesson from Lawrence: "the short, compact subject, made personal." He conceals the fact that he already knows Spain in order to concentrate on an effect of "the instantaneous and 'first sight' of the object"—an "infatuation" that was to dominate all his future writing in fiction and criticism.

At seventy Pritchett is not sorry that *Marching Spain* has been out of print for forty years: though the feeling was vigorous and original, the writing was still too "baroque." He had finished the writing in London and quickly found a publisher, Victor Gollancz. Though the book sold only six hundred copies, it attracted one parody and a reasonable number of reviews, one of which described him as "a genius with a brain packed in ice." Pritchett recalls the phrase as "a near miss": "I have talent, but no genius." He had indeed intended to give his images "a hard, icy, and brainy flash": again a formula that names a permanent quality of his vision and his style. When he attends his first publisher's party in Whitehall Court, where he knows no one present, he is glad to retreat from the crush and the shouted inanities to go out into the fog and read the Scotland Yard posters announcing Bodies Found, thence to walk home to his "cheese-flavoured room" in Fitzroy Street.

Gradually the patches come together into a wearable fabric, within which survival seems a probability. Pritchett begins regular reviewing for the *Monitor*, the *New Statesman*, the *Spectator*. Because he cannot afford London he moves to a flint cottage in the hills above Marlow. His life has found its characteristic shape: "And so I became a literary journalist of highbrow tastes who lives in a country cottage because it is cheap and who divides his time between reviewing and doing his 'own work.'" His reviews he tries to make serious essays that will be collectible. His "own work" is travel books, short stories, novels. With the peculiar clarity and candor that are the most moving quality of his work, Pritchett looks back upon himself as he is about to take leave of youth and enter middle life.

> It is so hard to remember youth, simply because one loses dramatic interest in oneself. One is harsh; one is all sentiment. It is the time of friendships. I used to think of myself as more exposed than my friends, yet clearly I was not. At a moment when I felt wise an elderly and amused doctor said I looked like a bolting pony. A poet, older than myself, said I burned everything up, including myself. I was tame yet I was avid. I was shy and I was aggressive. Goodness knows what any young man is like except egotistical and perhaps fanatical. I was fanatical about writing: the word and the sentence were my religion; everything must be definite.

His apparently more stable new life is far from easy or serene. He suffers from the accumulated and continuing tension of years of strain, anxiety, overwork. In 1929 after a sun-soaked and unproductive trip to the south of France, Pritchett is on the verge of a serious breakdown: "I walked about with a knife sticking into my back by day; when I went to bed my nightmares were about air warfare. I was often sitting with the crowd of Out Patients at hospitals, waiting to be X-rayed. My duodenum twanged. I went into fevers." What finally cured him, he notes simply, was "success"—in love and in work.

Beyond this point Pritchett says little about his writing. He treats his second marriage, which is what he meant by "love," also briefly but with his special brand of dry lyricism. The Irish marriage, flawed from the start, had gradually drifted into outright separation. There had been little love in it, and Pritchett awaited the *coup de foudre* that would awaken his heart. At the first sight of Dorothy in 1934 "strange tears" came into his eyes. They were married after his divorce in 1936. He finds his fully realized sexual passion a liberation and a firming, attributing to it frankly both the flowering of his talent and the dawning of his sense of responsibility, a general rounding of maturity.

The last quarter of *Midnight Oil* loops back to complete the story of the Pritchett parents. On his return from Spain in the middle twenties he had found them living in unwonted state in a villa in Bromley, with a maid and a chauffeur, the latter wisely provided by the Divine Mind of Christian Science, Pritchett surmises: his father had been a murderous driver. Yet though there are Turkish carpets and a grand piano, the general air of the furniture is still that of class warfare: "Oak, walnut, cherry, mahogany, flashed their veneers sarcastically at one another." The widowed Yorkshire grandmother has come to live out her last two years with them, nursed by her despised daughter-in-law. When she dies Walter Pritchett cannot bring himself to carry out her funeral, and the body lies in the house day after day. Pritchett describes the Gogolesque scene in brutal brief phrases: "The result was horror. The dead woman's body burst in the coffin and was borne dripping from the bedroom." None of the Pritchett children can feel any faith in the family prosperity, and indeed the business that had "so beglamoured and harassed" their lives soon falls into liquidation. Pritchett calls for the last time on his father in his dismantled office, shaken by pity and the shame of his own powerlessness. The ensuing scene eventually provided him with a complete short story:

> His office and factory were his real home, where he had kept so many things private to himself: his Gramophone, his photographs, his special coffee cups, the motto containing words of Emerson's. I feared we would both weep; we were saved by a distraction. A large fly flew in from the showroom. Father detested flies: emissaries of dirt. He went at it with a copy of *The Draper's Record*. I went at it with an evening paper. We missed. A fury seized us. He got up on his desk to bash it on the ceiling and there, looking down at me, he said sternly: "You're going bald, my boy."

Both the elder Pritchetts live into their eighties, and they have another fifteen years to go, a period which their son handles quickly and anecdotally, watching the jockeying rivalry of the old comedy run itself out on a diminished scale. Mrs. Pritchett makes herself a dozen pairs of bloomers out of heavy ornate stuffs left over from the drapery business, and models them with shrieks of laughter. Her husband finds nearly four hundred pounds that she has squirreled away over the years under a carpet and between layers of bed linen. She grows obsessed with the notion that she has cancer and lies for hours on a sofa rubbing her belly, eventually wearing holes in all her skirts. But it is Walter Pritchett who actually dies of cancer, undiagnosed, with shocking suddenness. His wife had gone first, and V. S. Pritchett marvels at the ramshackle dignity of her history: "In place of hope in her life, Mother wavered between fear and a sustaining sense of farce." Her habitual half-hysterical gaiety is what stays in his mind, and the way "everything turned into a tale in her talk—a tale she would tell, with her despairing work-worn fingers spread over her face, with her laughing eyes peering through the gaps between."

The passage is striking, in context, because it makes one of the comparatively rare occasions when Pritchett lets himself go to express outright a specified emotion of his own. The main impressions a reader takes away from his two volumes are those of courage, vitality, clarity, reserve. Those are properties of both subject and style; one need not labor to document them: they are audible everywhere in the language. Both subject and style, furthermore, are properties of temperament. One is impressed both by what is there and by what is left out. Pritchett strikes me as a very tough and intelligent man who survived a long deep wounding. The wound and the bow: he has been to hell and come back to tell about it—up to a point. In his first thirty years Pritchett took on a great deal of scar tissue, and I suspect he chose to treat it as a protective second skin.

All lives are hard but Pritchett's was harder than most. His family created him and by their lights nurtured him, but they very nearly killed him. England, France, Ireland, Spain gave him nothing willingly; they relinquished only what he was hard enough to seize. Writing, like going to the toilet, is something one must do for oneself, but few writers can have been so utterly self-made. Pritchett learned to write by reading and writing. No master, no old boys, pulled him along. The whole process, in life and art, left him tight-lipped—in art; that we do not really learn how he is in life is precisely the problem. Pritchett's reticence is English but it is also profoundly personal, exceptional even for an Englishman. It strikes me not as stoicism but as a strongly developed instinct for privacy, not less prickly for being unstated. We hear, unstated, a gritty murmur: "Certain things are none of your damned business."

Revolted by the vanity and self-pity that make so much of current fiction, poetry, and even criticism unreadable, one is embarrassed to complain of reticence when it occurs. But the "laconic," the "definite," so rare and ordinarily so admirable, can turn into a dangerous virtue when the subject, inescapably, is the self. We don't need any more egos but we can use any number of lives, if they have been useful ones, like Pritchett's, and if we are allowed far enough inside to understand the working of motive and feeling. Pritchett does not allow us very far inside. His very reticence, when frankly applied to a permitted moment of emotion, such as the death of his mother, can create a stunning little point-blank effect: "She lay, a tiny figure, so white and frail that she looked no more than a cobweb. I stood there hard and unable to weep. Tears come to me only at the transition from unhappiness to happiness; now I was frozen at the thought of her life. She had been through so much and I had been so outside it." It bothers one, however, that the effect is in a significant degree an effect of style, a triumph of withheld climax allowed to shock an established reserve, taking much of its power from its rarity.

I do not think Pritchett is hostile or immune to strong feeling; but it is hard to be sure, and that is exactly the difficulty I have with the matter. Late in *Midnight Oil* he remarks almost in passing: "It is pretty certain that the effect of the violent quarrels in my childhood home was to close my heart for a long time." Perhaps these and other traumas in the hardship of his life really did freeze Pritchett's heart. I do not think so; I think his heart simply got so sore that he did not want to talk about it; but I do not know, and my uncertainty makes me uncomfortable. In another of his dense little throwaway lines he speaks of "the supreme pleasure of putting oneself in by leaving oneself out." One knows what he means, and honors it; but in autobiography it does make a problem. Pritchett trusts us too far to find the self in the understatement and the withholding. We come to know a personality but not really a whole person. I prefer Frank O'Connor's way of letting his heart hang out, so long as he does not caress it too much—as he does not.

None of this makes me think Pritchett's books less than superb. Nobody in years has talked so clearly and wisely about the craft of writing and what might be called the moral psychology of the writer. What he does choose to give us of his life is so rich in texture and so sharp in specification that we are glad to forgive him a willed reservation.

The Teller's Own Tale
The Memoirs of Frank O'Connor

In turning from the autobiographical writing of the Englishman V. S. Pritchett to that of the Irishman Frank O'Connor (as I have done, in an experimental spirit) one enters a subtly but distinctly different world. Both men start at the bottom and raise themselves to eminence, but they perform in very different theaters of action. Pritchett passes through Ireland and acquires an unsatisfactory wife and a secondhand car there, but essentially he is a citizen of the great world, a cockney Englishman who achieves a real penetration of European culture. For O'Connor, Ireland, a sullenly subjected fief of England, still basically medieval in organization and temper, is the world, the limit of his horizon—so far as his two volumes carry his story. He is never anything but an inspired provincial.

The decisive differences are more personal and more interesting. They are matters of tone, tempo, texture, coloring. In the long run we can only call them matters of feeling: a difference in style that becomes literary but begins in temperament. One can sense the change in climate in O'Connor's first sentences in *An Only Child*. Blarney Lane in Cork, the scene of his first memories, he writes, "begins at the foot of Shandon Street . . . in sordidness, and ascends the hill to something like squalor." Or his first attempt to distinguish the strains in his genetic heritage: "One of the things I have inherited from my mother's side of the family is a passion for gaiety. I do not have it myself—I seem to take more after my father's family, which was brooding, melancholy, and violent—but I love gay people and books and music." This is the writing of a man who is genuinely, humbly, and humorously interested in the phenomenon of himself. Primarily what we feel is greater intimacy and less strain as compared to Pritchett, a looser tension. O'Connor takes his data no less clinically than Pritchett, and he is at least as deeply wounded by his traumatic history, but he is less choked up, less insulted. Something—I am inclined to call it softness of heart—has freed him to respond more flexibly, with a larger swing of feeling. Both men are very witty, very funny; O'Connor is more authentically humorous: more forgiving, I suppose. (O'Connor the writer obviously does possess gaiety, though he thinks it recessive in his personality.) Pritchett's wit is sharp, spasmodic, retaliatory. O'Connor's may be equally sharp at last but it comes out more slowly, as the indulgent fermentation of the mind. It feels harder won, better earned; less nervous, more profound.

Intimacy, warmth, a frank vulnerability of the heart, then, and to me it is grateful after Pritchett's overcontrol. It is as if something limiting and permanent happened to Pritchett's reactive tissue, emotional and intellectual, when he saw the Castilian landscape that he treats as epiphany: that "geometry under a clear cold sky and dry winter sun," speaking to him of "the immediate and finite, so much more satisfying than the infinite." There, Pritchett says, "one began to see exactly." But the event did not occur entirely from the outside; it happened because Pritchett's temperament as an individual and an Englishman required and craved it. The disposition to a sharpening and limiting objectivity already existed, waiting a model and an energy. Thenceforward the writer sought quick accuracy, stripped statement: "the laconic," "the instantaneous and 'first sight' of the object," images that emit a "hard, icy, and brainy flash." The kind of flashing vision that follows from such trained cerebration can be intensely exciting to the reader, but in the long run it turns a little chilling. One feels instructed, even rearranged, by Pritchett's intelligent English reticence, but also undernourished, hungry for fuller feeling.

Perhaps the wet green mounded landscape of Ireland did not encourage the Castilian refrigeration; the hazy air proposed a softer steeping. But such things happen because the national and personal temper predisposes, makes ready. As English reticence can be chilling, so Irish emotionalism can be cloying, overfilling, too thick on the tongue unless controlled by O'Connor's kind of acidity and sane deprecation. But the deeper differences between these two writers are more individual than they are national. Ultimately they go back to the extraordinary tensions of the home.

The Pritchett domesticity might be called violently extroverted: populous, contentious, shifting, incoherent. It has no stability, no center emotionally, morally, or intellectually. In the midst of the hectic activity nothing moves that can be called simply love. To survive that chaos, an intelligent nature will isolate itself, damping down its responses, collecting and husbanding its resources against the day of freedom. Though he treats the idea unemphatically, Pritchett comes close to the heart of the matter when he remarks late in *Midnight Oil:* "It is pretty certain that the effect of the violent quarrels in my childhood home was to close my heart for a long time." In fact we never see his heart really opened, though he does tell us, in a sentence, that his heart was finally freed by "finding" his contemporaries and by "success in love." The details and the coloring of his liberation are apparently none of our business.

O'Connor's childhood was even more cruel than Pritchett's, but it was more bearable and more fertilizing, for within the cruelty and deprivation a love of the purest and warmest kind, between the son and the orphan charwoman mother, burned well into his middle years. The title of O'Connor's first volume, *An Only Child,* names a crucial difference between his experience and that of Pritchett: the family passions that are divided among four children in the Pritchett household bear upon a single small boy in O'Connor's case. The tense triangular relationship of mother, father, and child was lived out with a privacy, an intimacy, a delimitation of available view that was unknown to Pritchett. The life could never have been called stable, but at least the dimensions of its ghastliness were always visible and in a sense logical. The noisy dishevelment of Pritchett's childhood made him seek concentration, clarity. O'Connor's early loneliness made him wish to move outward, to lay his heart open genially to life.

O'Connor presents himself, as Pritchett does and as anyone must, as the unequally poised amalgam of two genetic strains—in his case as the only child of Minnie O'Connor and Michael O'Donovan. Such is his fear-hate-love of his father, half brute and half child, that the boy clings to the fantasy that he is a changeling, the child of his beloved mother and of a father unknown but surely preferable. Joyce might have called the senior Michael O'Donovan an imperfectly citified firbolg. He is a tall, strong, handsome, sentimental, stupid brute of a man, a Boer War veteran whose striking physique, according to his own story, had caught the eye of Victoria herself at a military review. He comes of peasant stock, and his mother, who shares the house for a time, is a stout slatternly woman of Mongolian appearance, steeped in porter and stockfish, coarse in feeding and speaking, slopping about in bare feet and shrugging her itching unwashed shoulders. O'Connor identifies his paternal line with "drunkenness, dirt, and violence." The navvy Mick O'Donovan is shy, proud, inarticulate; and he exercises over his wife and child the kind of mindless tyranny that gratifies a passionate unintelligent nature lacking any healthy vent. O'Connor remembers being suddenly set down from his father's knee so that O'Donovan can pick up the poker with which he has been mulling porter and slash his own brother across the face. He puts his wife and child into the street in their nightclothes, and they know it is not an empty threat when he waves his straight razor about in a drunken fury. Yet when he is not "on the drink" he is a steady, quiet, baffled, home-keeping man, and so fine a workman that he can always find a new job after one of his extended sprees. And he helplessly loves and needs his wife. But the boy also helplessly loves and needs her. The rivalry is real, the triangular affair only semicomic.

An Only Child is essentially a love story, the story of Frank O'Connor's pride in and love for his small, pretty, dark-haired mother, the person of finest grain in all the four books by the two autobiographers. She preserves her gaiety, her intelligence, her purity of feeling, her natural elegance in spite of the crushing bitterness of her life. After the death of her father, her impoverished mother is finally driven to place Minnie O'Connor and her sister Margaret in the Catholic orphanage of the Good Shepherd. Frank O'Connor describes the scene, one of the many reluctantly recounted to him by his mother over a period of years: "When Mother realized that they were being left behind, she rushed after my grandmother, clinging to her skirts and screaming to be taken home. My grandmother's whispered reply is one of the phrases that haunted my childhood—indeed, it haunts me still. 'But, my store, I have no home now.' For me, there has always been in imagination a stage beyond death—a stage where one says 'I have no home now.'" (The reflection of the last sentence, indeed the whole episode, is an example of the kind of thing V. S. Pritchett would likely feel was too emotional, too private to record.) Margaret is left crippled by a fever epidemic: "One day two girls entered the classroom, carrying a third whose legs dragged dead behind her. 'Minnie,' they said. 'Here's your sister.'"

Eventually Margaret dies in the orphanage, but Minnie grows to adolescence there and is then sent out to work as a housemaid in a series of increasingly terrible lower-middle-class households, usually Protestant, where she is bullied for her compliance and hated for her beauty, innocence, and high spirits. The worst of her mistresses, jealous and sadistic, reduces her to starvation and rags and forces her to cut off her beautiful long hair when it becomes lousy. Her condition O'Connor diagnoses bleakly as despair, and he addresses it in one of his acute little asides about human nature: "Children, and adolescents who have retained their childish innocence have little hold on life. They have no method of defending themselves against the things that are not in their own nature." At the point of suicide she is taken in by the nuns again, and soon she finds the place that was to give her eight happy years, the only benign interval in the first half of her life: the big house of Ned Barry, a prosperous bachelor, and his beautiful spinster sister Alice. (It is curiously exhilarating to meet in O'Connor's historical narrative such persons, forms of whom one has known as characters in his short stories.) The Barrys offer Minnie O'Connor not only kindness and gaiety but also love, and she lives with them, as much friend and confidante as servant, until Alice marries and the nuns force her to leave the now-unchaperoned house. Soon she is fatally married herself, to the crony of her soldier brother Tim, who warns her fruitlessly from South Africa: "Have nothing to do with Mick Donovan. He's a good friend, but he'll make a poor husband."

The central facts of domestic life are poverty and drink. The mother goes out as a charwoman at a shilling a day to supplement their small income. The little boy is much alone. Life is poor but tolerable, and evenings about the fire and the lamp in the wretched cottage are close and warm. It is not clear just what Mick O'Donovan earns, for he turns over only the bare minimum and puts the rest away in a trunk upstairs against a rainy day. The rainy day always proves to be a prolonged drunk that is shattering to all three. The savings in the trunk last a week or so; then the mother's trips to the pawnbroker begin: first Mick's blue suit, then the clock without the alarm, then his silver watch, then her blue suit, then his military medals, then his "ring paper" by which he draws his British army pension, and finally her wedding ring. He is unable to work of course, and he is "all day about the house, his head swollen, his eyes bloodshot, sitting by the fire and shivering in the fever of alcoholism . . . unable to think of anything except drink." When his wife returns home with her pitiful wage or the pawnbroker's allowance, he is off for a night's drinking. It all ends only when every source of credit is closed. Then "sour and savage and silent" he goes out to find a new job and gradually to pay off his debts and to recover, in reverse order, the pawned possessions; and the peaceful evenings by the fire recommence.

Why does she not leave the drunken brute? The little boy wonders, as the neighbors do. He is middle-aged himself before he understands: to free herself she would have had to become a housekeeper and put her child in an orphanage, and Minnie O'Connor had had enough of orphanages. More intimately she was moved by pity, "pity for this giant of a man who had no more self-knowledge or self-control than a baby," this mental and spiritual invalid the two sides of whose nature "hardly communicated and were held together by pins and Hail Marys"; and moved moreover by gratitude: years later, holding his mother's hand as she mutters in a serious illness, O'Connor hears her whisper, "God! God! He raised me from the gutter where the world threw me." (Walter Pritchett had reversed the direction of that formula: "I raised you from the gutter.") The marriage was to last as long as life. O'Connor carries the long first section of his book down to his mother's old age, when she is denied by his own children outside the courtroom where his visiting rights as father are being defined, and to his intensely moving farewell tribute:

> When she was dead, and I had done all the futile things she would have wished, like bringing her home across the sea to rest with Father, and when the little girl who had refused to speak to her in court had knelt beside the coffin in the luggage van at Kingsbridge, and the little boy had joined the train at Limerick Junction, I returned to the house she had left. When she fell ill, I had been teaching the child who was left me a Negro spiritual, and now when we came home together and I opened the front door, he felt that everything was going to be the same again and that we could go back to our singing. He began, in a clear treble: "Child, I know you're going to miss me when I'm gone." Then only did I realize that the horror that had haunted me from the time I was his age and accompanied Mother to the orphanage, and learned for the first time the meaning of parting and death, had happened at last to me, and that it made no difference to me that I was fifty and a father myself.
>
> And I await the resurrection from the dead and eternal life to come.

One who has come to know Minnie O'Connor through her son's loving recollections will read the passage with misty eyes. Whereas Pritchett may have felt such emotions, so far above self or shame, he never shares them with us, and I feel that is a loss.

Though the fact seems hardly possible, O'Connor's education is even patchier and stranger than Pritchett's. In fact it is almost entirely his own creation. He does not resist education; he hankers after it with the kind of dreamy passion that Pritchett would call transcendental. The boy O'Connor believes absolutely what he has been told, that education is "necessary": "You could get nowhere without education." But what and where was the stuff? At the level on which the O'Donovans lived it was hard to know. The lad's vision of education is also hopelessly clouded by the English boys' penny weeklies, the *Gem* and the *Magnet*, which provided the Invisible Presences that enrich and confuse his boyhood. So he "adored education from afar, and strove to be worthy of it," and went on shadow-boxing before the mirror in the kitchen, practicing the deadly straight left with which the hero periodically gave the bully of the school what was coming to him. Meanwhile he is moving in somnambular fashion through the parroting recitations and the brutalities of the rod that Cork City offers as education for a poor Catholic child of vivid imagination.

It is not till Daniel Corkery becomes his master that he gets a first tentative taste of authentic intellectual and political passion. Being "a natural collaborationist," going "a bit of the road with everybody" like Dolan's ass, feeling "love" for Corkery, and imitating, as was his lifelong habit, anyone he loved, young O'Connor is soon imitating Corkery. In practice this meant learning rags and tags of anything more or less genuinely native Irish: language, literature, legend, history. As far as the school authorities are concerned, this is only another mode of dreaming. His masters declare him a boy who will never pass examinations and order him placed in the trade school. Here he is even more hopelessly bored and lost, and by the age of fourteen Frank O'Connor has given up school altogether. He has concluded that any education he is to get must be self-administered, so "with the rest of the unemployed" he haunts the Carnegie Library to read and to scan advertisements for "a smart boy," hoping for a job that will let him buy the books in which he can "pick up" an education. Successively and disastrously he works in the shops of a draper, a chemist, and a printer, and for a longer spell as a messenger boy in the railway freight warehouse, where he is known as "the Native" because he can speak some Irish, where he pursues "1 Bale Foreskins" in all innocence, and in general proves himself hopelessly inept—not a smart boy.

Meanwhile, painfully and passionately, "an education" is being scraped together. With wider reading the dream school-world of the English boys' weeklies is gradually undermined, and in a final fantasy that reads like a Jack Yeats watercolor O'Connor bids them a grateful farewell: "One day I woke to find the Invisible Presences of my childhood departing with a wave of the hand as they passed forever from sight. Not angrily, nor even reproachfully, but sadly, as good friends part." An eager mind can find fertility in astonishing kinds of trash, for example the lumber room of a house where Minnie cleans: "Chock full of treasures—old pamphlets, guide books, phrase books in French and German, school books . . . old dance programmes from Vienna and Munich that contained musical illustrations of Schubert's songs, and . . . an illustrated book of the Oberammergau Passion Play with the text in German and English." Such junk served Frank O'Connor as "the right twigs for an eagle's nest." He is fascinated with anything to do with literature, language, painting, music. He buys a Self-Educator and raids the Carnegie Library with his mother's card. Having learned from Canon Sheehan's novels that "German was the real language of culture and that the greatest of cultured persons was Goethe," he reads "right through" Goethe in English and studies German in the Self-Educator in order to be able to read him in the original.

At the outset, of course, such learning is a makeshift illusory affair: as he puts it, "I learned only by pretending to know." With no knowledge of the structural principles of any language, even English, and before he has even heard, for example, of Browning, the boy works entirely by eye and ear, and he soon knows by heart thousands of lines in Irish and German which he could have translated only imperfectly. To the mature O'Connor, the period returns "as a hallucination rather than as a memory." It was a weirdly divided life, in which the body inhabited one world, and the mind, in its pathetically few hours of freedom, another world of pastiche that still was necessary and ultimately salvatory. The boy reads his first paper to the Gaelic League the same night he is discharged from the railway. As he looks at the polite attentive faces of his elders little less ignorant than himself, he has a sudden clear vision of the absurdity of his situation:

> While I was speaking, it was suddenly borne in on me that I no longer had a job or a penny in the world, or even a home I could go back to without humiliation, and that the neighbours would say, as they had so often said before, that I was mad and a good-for-nothing. And I knew that they would be right, for here I was committing myself in public to all the vague words and vaguer impressions that with me passed for thought.

Absurd or not, he is committed: "I had tossed my cap over the wall of life, and I knew I must follow it, wherever it had fallen." He had already become what he would always be, a self-taught provincial intellectual of genius.

By now Ireland is into her troubles. The Easter Rising of 1916 has come and gone, but political unrest continues. As O'Connor sees the matter, the country was "improvising" a revolution as he was improvising an education, and in both cases "it was the make-believe that succeeded." Life in Cork proceeds with the brilliant bitterness that is peculiar to Ireland. The lord mayor is shot in his own house in front of his wife. His successor, Terence MacSwiney, is arrested and starves himself to death in a London jail. One night the whole center of the city goes up in flames. Frank O'Connor had made one of those who filed past to look at MacSwiney's "long, dark, masochistic face" as he lay in his coffin in City Hall; and in spite of his youth and his father's disapproval he puts together a patchy facsimile of a Volunteer uniform, and buys and carries home, down the leg of his trousers, a French rifle for which there is not a round of ammunition in Ireland.

He applies for and receives a scholarship to a summer school in Dublin run by the Gaelic League to train hedge-schoolmasters, teachers of Irish who were to travel by bicycle from one village to another. Shy and practically penniless, he lives on coffee and buns in Bewley's as he stumbles through his training. He is "qualified," however, and practices his mystery in country schoolrooms for a few weeks until he is prevented by the curfew. His circle of friends is widening outside that of his old neighborhood streetlamp, and he falls in love for the first time; but he suffers agonies of ineptitude and shyness: "I always talked too much, usually lost control of myself, and heard myself say things that were ridiculous, false, or base, and afterwards remained awake, raging and sobbing by turns as I remembered every detail of my own awkwardness, lying, and treachery." There lies the germ of his wonderfully funny and touching story "Judas." His father refuses to grant him maturity and still goes through his ritual locking-up, "the latch, the lock, the big bolt, and the little bolt," every night at ten o'clock whether the young man has come home or not: the germ of "The Procession of Life," in which a callow young man is thrown on the wicked city at night by being locked out of his house.

In the summer of 1921 comes the truce that ended seven centuries of English occupation, in the following winter the treaty, and, on the heels of that, civil war between the Free Staters who accepted the treaty and the Republicans who held out for an independent republic to include Ulster—neither side understanding, O'Connor says bitterly, that what they were about to create was "a new Establishment of Church and State in which imagination would play no part, and young men and women would emigrate to the ends of the earth, not because the country was poor, but because it was mediocre." Frank O'Connor "took the Republican side because it was Corkery's."

Being a literary lad (still in his teens) he is named a "war correspondent," a sort of propagandizing reporter for the Republican cause, and the field of vision in his memoir immediately expands and turns anarchic. His view of the "improvised" Irish revolution, like Pritchett's but better earned, is basically comic. Though his coloring darkens as his canvas enlarges, he generally treats the slapdash affair with the kind of ironic deprecation he has been applying to himself all along. The Republicans have a Particularly Fierce Armored Car, and a little cannon that the inventor has brought down from Dublin with nine shells: he is still working on the tenth. The "front line," which nobody can quite locate anyway, is abandoned while the soldiers go to Mass.

It seems a toy war, yet the issue is real and the bloodshed is real, and copious enough once the ambushes and executions get under way and the "real killers" emerge on both sides. Nothing is more deadly than Irish deadliness, the firbolg cruelty, chthonic and implacable. O'Connor can accept clean killing, but he is appalled by the instinct for brutality he feels around him. One morning he is told that he is needed for a "job" that evening: "to shoot unarmed soldiers courting their girls in deserted laneways, and the girls as well if there was any danger of our being recognized." In outrage he goes to protest to Mary MacSwiney, sister of the dead lord mayor and the local representative in parliament: "She received me very coldly. She thought me an indiscreet young man, which, indeed, I was. 'You seem to have some moral objection to killing women,' she said disapprovingly, and when I admitted that I had, she added complacently: 'I see no *moral* objection, though there may be a *political* one.'" (One recalls his great story "Guests of the Nation.") Happily the operation was called off. After his second and conclusive capture by the Free Staters, O'Connor is taken to view another prisoner who is awaiting execution and who has been beaten with rifle butts and "skewered through the ass with bayonets." The apparition was to haunt him for years: "The battered face of that boy was something that wasn't in any book, and even ten years later, when I was sitting reading in my flat in Dublin, the door would suddenly open and he would walk in and the book would fall from my hands."

Of O'Connor's record of the war the most baffling and intriguing pages, to him and to his reader, are those that treat the senior Erskine Childers (father of the late Irish prime minister), a British army officer with Irish family connections, who had written a famous prophetic thriller, *The Riddle of the Sands,* had helped carry out the gunrunning at Howth for the Volunteers in July 1914, and who now, with the Great War finished, came back to Ireland to serve the Republican cause. "The damned Englishman" has been marked for death by the Free State forces, even though their formidable commander, Michael Collins, is his friend and is said to have given him the little .22 revolver he wears pinned "like a flower" to his suspenders under his outer clothing. To O'Connor he is the arch-incongruity in the deadly comedy of the struggle, a man with no reason to be there, yet absolutely there. Childers seems to have distilled away all egotism and even self-consciousness, to be a man reduced to pure abstract purpose. He is finally captured with the little gun that justifies his execution, and spends his last night playing chess with his cousin, taken with him, using improvised equipment through a chink in the wall of their adjoining cells. O'Connor, who had met him often but found his preoccupation impossible to penetrate, conceives the scene of his execution in an act of pure imaginative sympathy:

> I have had to go through those last few terrible moments with him almost as though I were there: see the slight figure . . . emerge for the last time into the Irish daylight, apparently cheerful and confident but incapable of grandiose gestures, concerned only lest inadvertently he might do or say something that would distress some poor fool of an Irish boy who was about to level an English rifle at his heart.

The year and a half terminating in the spring of 1923 is a period O'Connor finds almost too painful to recall. For the most part he spends it dodging about the vicinity of Cork, still penniless, and essentially homeless now as he dares not sleep in his own house. When he is captured "effortlessly one morning by two Free State soldiers," he is fortunately unarmed, so he is sent off to make one of a thousand Republican prisoners in a former American airdrome north of Dublin. The year he spends there is by no means unhappy: the serious fighting is about over; he need not struggle to live; the American plumbing is a revelation; the lonely boy who likes company has plenty of it. He begins to teach Irish to other prisoners and soon German as well, and he discovers grammar: "For me, languages had always been a form of magic, like girls." It is an epiphany comparable to George Moore's famous discovery of the subjunctive, and he undertakes a lifelong love affair with grammar. He also begins to find absurdity in some of his supposed political principles, and to act with a new independence, at one point joining two other men who refuse to accompany the other 997 prisoners in a hunger strike.

When he returns home, dazed by freedom, his mother bursts into tears and exclaims, "It made a man of you": she is both impressed and chagrined. Though O'Connor has frequently attacked the "introverted" religion of Ireland in *An Only Child,* he is far from irreligious. At the end of the book he is brooding upon the immortality of the soul: a condition for which he is sure he cannot qualify, though others, particularly his mother, do qualify. As his whole book has been an act of worship of his mother, he ends with a paean to her, cast appropriately in the scriptural terms that always occur to him when he is thinking of her in a comprehensive way:

I knew that there were souls that were immortal, that even God, if He wished to, could not diminish or destroy, and perhaps it was the thought of these that turned me finally from poetry to story-telling, to the celebration of those who for me represented all I should ever know of God. My mother was merely one among them, though, in my human weakness, I valued her most, and now that I am old myself, I remember the line of a psalm (probably mistranslated) that has always been with me since I read it first:
"And when I wake I shall be satisfied with Thy likeness."

Because O'Connor left his second memoir, *My Father's Son*, incomplete when he died in March 1966, it is impossible to judge the work with any decisiveness. Maurice Sheehy of University College, Dublin, "compared the different drafts and produced the present text," according to the publisher's note. I take this to mean that the writing is O'Connor's, the organization basically Sheehy's. One cannot know how much further writing or rewriting O'Connor meant to do; all one can say is that both men have made a good job of the matter, and the book as it stands reads very well indeed. The scene quite naturally, as in Pritchett's second volume, is less dramatic and enclosed, more expansive in space and time, more professional in concerns than the first. Michael and Minnie O'Donovan are still much on their son's mind, but the basic story is that of his years as a librarian, a man of the theater, and an outsetting writer: an inhabitant of an Irish literary world, situated reluctantly in Dublin in the main, rather than in Cork. Like that of *An Only Child*, the style is modest, musing, humorous, even more anecdotal and filled with "characters."

Still only twenty, and still penniless and wearing his father's old trousers, the "ex-jailbird" learns late in 1923 that the playwright Lennox Robinson, as secretary of the Irish Carnegie United Kingdom Trust, is hiring young men to be trained as librarians for new provincial libraries. He finds Robinson drinking double brandies in the Cork railway station and is taken on at the munificent salary of thirty shillings a week. He goes off to Sligo for his apprenticeship carrying a cardboard suitcase containing his spare shirt and underpants and a few pairs of stockings knit by his mother. When he has paid for his lodgings, he has "a whole half-crown for laundry, cigarettes, and drink"; but he is happy enough with an inexhaustible supply of books. When he is summoned to London for a conference, it is his first trip outside Ireland; crossing the Irish Sea he lies awake all night, seasick and reciting *Lycidas* for consolation.

After six months in Sligo, O'Connor crosses the island to Wicklow to serve in the new county library as assistant to Geoffrey Phibbs, an

English-educated Anglo-Irishman, a poet and a tempestuous lover of poetry who becomes a dear friend. It is through Phibbs that O'Connor forms the crucial friendship of his dawning career as a writer. The two go to Dublin to protest a slighting reference in the *Irish Statesman* and find the editor, George William Russell (Æ), in his attic in Merrion Square lined with brown paper that he has painted with his characteristic gods and goddesses and other subjects from his visionary imagination: "a big, burly North of Ireland Presbyterian with wild hair and beard and a pipe hanging from his discoloured teeth." Phibbs says to Russell: "The difference between your generation and ours is that we have had no youth." When Russell replies, "Oh, really!" O'Connor "disgraces" himself with a shout of laughter in which Russell joins, and from that moment the two men are friends. Russell invites him to "send me something for the paper."

Since it was understood that all of Russell's "discoveries" must be vetted by W. B. Yeats, O'Connor waits upon the great man at one of his Monday evenings. He describes the elegant strange figure that daunted so many: "The tall man in the well-cut blue suit with the silk shirt and bow-tie who came shuffling in, holding his hand out high as though he expected you to kiss his ring—a beautiful ring, as it happened. . . . There was something ecclesiastical about the blind man's stare, the ceremonial washing of the hands and the languid unction of the voice." In time O'Connor recognizes that it is shyness as well as poor eyesight that gives a spasmodic quality to Yeats's social presence; he soon recognizes as well the love of deviousness and the malice, and the formidable intelligence with its strong practical side. Both Yeats and Russell are men of genius, in O'Connor's view. But Yeats's ruthlessness leaves his genius freer to function; Russell's is enmeshed in busyness and personal kindness:

> Within half an hour he enveloped you in universal curiosity and affection in which shyness was forgotten. It was like an old fur coat, a little bit smelly and definitely designed for someone of nobler stature, but, though it might threaten you with suffocation, it never left you feeling cold. He would find you a new doctor, a new wife, a new lodging, a new job, and if you were ill would cheerfully come and nurse you.

In the simplest of his formulas O'Connor distinguishes between the two men: "Yeats loved the half light, Russell the full light." O'Connor admires and loves them both; in the long run it is Yeats he admires the more, Russell he loves the more.

Drawn back by love for his mother and for his native city, and acting against the advice of Russell, O'Connor takes the post of librarian for Cork County at a salary of £250 a year: "great money; more than anyone in Harrington's Square had ever earned." For the next two years he goes about his bookish business, struggling with parish priests who see libraries as instruments of ungodliness and county councilmen who see them as a God-given mechanism for lining their pockets. He is beginning to understand "the real Ireland, lonely and dotty," that would form the subject matter of his brilliant stories soon to come: "This was no longer the romantic Ireland of the little cottages and the hunted men, but an Ireland where everyone was searching frantically for a pension or a job."

But he is restless for the literary society of Phibbs and Russell and Yeats, and when a post opens for a municipal librarian in a Dublin suburb he takes it gladly. He proposes to buy a house on the Dublin coast for himself and his parents, but again his father will not hear of the idea, though he does generously allow Minnie to come to Dublin for extended visits. O'Connor's other loves for the moment are his distinguished elders. That tendency to form emotional relationships with older men he also labels as a weakness of "the Mother's Boy." The process had begun for him with Daniel Corkery when he was a schoolboy, and it continues now with Russell and Yeats. His picture of Russell is long and circumstantial, and he brings him to life as no one else has, penetrating to the passion and power of mind thickly overlaid with habit and junk learning and a fatal affinity for abstraction. O'Connor carries us through Russell's exasperated friendship with Yeats, his amused spectatorship of the jockeying rivalries of the famous Celtic scholars of the period—Kuno Meyer, Osborn Bergin, T. F. O'Rahilly, and others—through the excruciating scenes in Russell's house where he is handing out his treasures of books and pictures before he goes off to London to die of cancer, and on to his graveside where it is young O'Connor who delivers a parting address.

Two years later, in 1937, O'Connor undergoes what he calls a dress rehearsal of the death that had terrified him prospectively since childhood: his mother's. On his father's insistence he had searched out the orphan's birth record at the Customs House and found that she was exactly seventy years old. Thinking to celebrate her first known birthday, he brings home a bottle of champagne; overstimulated, she tumbles down a flight of stairs, breaking her shoulder and her pelvis. The two doctors who treat her (discovering in the process that she has suffered silently all her life with chronic appendicitis) predict that she cannot survive; but with devoted nursing by her son she does recover, and in fact lives on for another fifteen years. It is Michael O'Donovan who dies, in the early days of the war. Frank O'Connor had taken a wife himself by now, a divorced woman with a young son, and shamed and despairing, he had turned his father away when he arrived in Dublin for a visit in a drunken state. He was never to see him alive again:

> He had died as he had lived, blundering drunk about Cork in the last stages of pneumonia, sustained by nothing but his giant physique. . . . Mother refused to tell me anything until he was dead. This was something I found hard to forgive, because though with half her mind she felt she was saving me anxiety, deep down there was something else, not far removed from resentment—the feeling that I wouldn't understand and that I never had understood. She was like a loving woman who, when her husband has been unfaithful to her, blames not the husband, but the other woman. "That damned drink!" she would cry bitterly, always implying that it was the drink that followed Father, not Father the drink, and in this she was probably wiser than I. But she felt that only she could have the patience to deal with him when he was dying and to realize that he must be allowed to die in his own way, not mine, as in later years she followed him with Masses and prayers, knowing as no one else could know, how lost and embarrassed that shy, home-keeping man would be with no Minnie O'Connor to come home to, no home, no Cork, no pension, astray in the infinite wastes of eternity.

The final quarter of *My Father's Son* centers upon W. B. Yeats and the Abbey Theatre and tells a story of confusion and decay and bootless conspiracy that leaves one wondering how the institution survived at all. Yet it is material of great fascination and historical importance. O'Connor is introduced to the Abbey and its mines and countermines by the "brilliant, moody, despondent" Lennox Robinson, "Lennix" to Yeats: the talented, obstructive, and self-destructive drunkard who had drifted into control with the death of Lady Gregory and Yeats's preoccupation with other affairs. The theater is heavily in debt and is kept going mainly by the brilliance with which a group of veteran actors—Barry Fitzgerald, F. J. McCormick, Eileen Crowe, Maureen DeLaney—handle a set of established native comedies. Before long O'Connor has been invited to join the board himself.

His sometimes acrimonious friendship with Yeats continues and grows more complex. He taunts Yeats for his deviousness as Yeats taunts him for his naïveté. (Oliver St. John Gogarty had attacked O'Connor cruelly at a dinner of the Irish Academy as "a country boy with hair in his nose and hair in his ears and a brief-case in his hand.") It takes him a long time to realize that though Yeats is busy and ill and seemingly detached, the theater is still to him the most important thing in the work of his life, a sacred legacy from himself, Synge, and Lady Gregory to be preserved and passed on to the nation. Again and again O'Connor is startled by an example of Yeats's genius as a practical man of the theater. At the same time he is amused and touched to see the expeditiousness with which Yeats turns quotidian matter into lyric poetry. O'Connor had upbraided the director Hugh Hunt who on "English" naturalistic principles had allowed a young actress to sob intermittently during the long final speech of the old queen in Lady Gregory's *Dervorgilla*. When he reports the disagreement to Yeats and asks his opinion as to whether an actor should ever sob before the final curtain, Yeats snaps: "Never." When O'Connor sees the printed poem "Lapis Lazuli," he is astonished to see that their conversation had got incorporated into Yeats's extraordinary definition of tragic emotion in which he asserts that "Hamlet and Lear are gay; / Gaiety transfiguring all that dread":

> Yet they, should the last scene be there,
> The great stage curtain about to drop,
> If worthy their prominent part in the play,
> Do not break up their lines to weep.

The memorable scenes toward the end of *My Father's Son* are likely to be bitter ones: Yeats toiling up the stairs to the board room, pausing every two or three steps to collect enough breath to move on; Yeats presiding at the board meeting in which he must admit that his old friend Lennox Robinson must go for the good of the institution. Light moments are few now, as O'Connor's dissatisfaction with his life approaches saturation, but they too can be vivid: George Yeats seeing him to the door after he has squabbled all evening with her husband, doing a dance step in the hall, and exulting: "That old bully! It's about time someone stood up to him. He's always trying to push people around."

It is easier to stand up to cantankerous brilliance than to mediocrity—which, as O'Connor defines it, "having neither thesis nor antithesis, leads only a sort of biological life": being essentially shapeless, mediocrity offers its enemy no handhold. With the passing of Yeats in 1939 Ireland's great day in the arts was coming to an end. The imaginative genius and general distinction of mind of Yeats and his generation had been a miracle, not genetically transmissible. The Day of the Rabblement had come. In O'Connor's view the anesthetic of "the Nationalist-Catholic establishment" was permeating the cultural life of Ireland, and he was too bored and disenchanted to contend with it. Finally he decides to take Harold Macmillan's advice and set up as a full-time writer: once more he throws his cap over the wall of life and follows it. We follow him, gratefully.

Four Winds

I

Reading Donald Davie's attractive review of Donald Hall's *Remembering Poets* in the *New York Times Book Review* gave me a quick case of déjà vu. It came over me that I too had met Mr. Hall's stars, and in the same order: Dylan Thomas, Robert Frost, T. S. Eliot, Ezra Pound. Furthermore, though only the Thomas episode involved aught of the spectacular, all of my encounters were characteristic and interesting—worth setting down and passing on, I felt, if only to add to the available data of personality.

It is odd, in fact, for me to have met these four poets, for I don't move much in literary society, and I have a crotchety prejudice, sometimes stupid in its workings, against writers as public figures, as celebrities—a pose that destroyed Thomas and badly damaged Auden. I missed Edith Sitwell, for example, when she put on a great show at Mount Holyoke, because I had got her name twisted in my head with that of another poet I had no wish to hear; and I boycotted all of William Faulkner's public appearances in Charlottesville because I took against the atmosphere of display and jealousy, of mine and countermine, that had accumulated about his presence there. But I pretend no general immunity to the appeal of great folk in the flesh.

During 1949–1950, after academic beginnings too complex and dull to review here, I was teaching English at Smith College in Northampton, Massachusetts, while my wife, Jane, was teaching at Mount Holyoke, ten miles away in South Hadley. Our home was a former farmhouse in the village of Williamsburg, and it was from there that we drove over to South Hadley to hear Dylan Thomas on a damp chilly evening early in March 1950 with a foot or so of dirty crystalline snow on the ground. We were accompanied by my longtime friend Jerry Myers, then teaching philosophy at Smith, younger than I at twenty-five but a veteran madcap, always alert for larks. When we entered Pratt Hall, a few minutes before the scheduled hour of eight o'clock, we were met at the door by one of the locals who jibed: "Ha ha, you Smith types—Thomas isn't here yet, but he's somewhere on the way from Harvard. Why don't you go have a drink and come back in an hour or so?" We learned later that according to a telegram from Cambridge, Thomas had been mysteriously in transit since 3:30 in the afternoon; but he had not appeared for dinner or for anything else, and the audience had been sent home and advised to await developments. Our little party drove a couple of miles south to the Halfway House, drank beer and dawdled, and returned to Pratt.

By pure luck we had hit it just right. We strolled up to the front door, cold sober, precisely at the moment when Dylan Thomas was reeling and rolling in, urged along by the young man who had driven him over from Harvard—an odd type he still seems, nameless and noncommittal, too old for an undergraduate, too straight for a graduate student, neat and drab, unspeaking and apparently uninterested. He must have been the nearest man with a car at the last hysterical moment in Cambridge.

At that time my knowledge of Thomas's writing was probably limited to the solid selection of early poems in Oscar Williams's *Little Treasury of Modern Poetry*, where, among the oval medallions of portrait photographs in the back, I had found one of my prepared images of the poet: plump, young, Celtic, and eager. I also knew the portrait by Augustus John, presenting a sort of strayed John the Baptist or a slightly bee-stung Botticelli angel. What one met in the vestibule of Pratt was a reject from Hals or Teniers, fat, flaming, and foul, a man ruined in his middle thirties. Dylan Thomas looked as if he had been rolled or kicked the hundred miles through the dirty snow from Cambridge. He sweated and stank and scratched; his little pig eyes swam in his mottled pig face. The body inside the rumpled filthy clothes looked not so much fat as inflated, pumped full of some unhealthy pasty matter. It was hard to tell what he was saying as he reeled and mumbled there in the lobby in a little circle of appalled English department sponsors, but one gradually made out that he needed a toilet beyond all things.

Left to myself I would have turned about and headed home, or at most have found a seat in the crowded auditorium humming beyond the closed doors and put my head on my knees. But my friend Jerry had scented a lark, and he hissed at me: "Come on!" He took possession of Thomas's left arm, I took his right, and we made a weaving march toward the basement stairs. Finding the men's room in a women's college is often a problem, but I knew there was one somewhere in the caverns under Pratt. Downstairs we went through a door in pitch dark, with no light switch to be found. There ensued a burlesque act in which we stumbled in troika, striking matches as we went, until we found the right door and pushed the needy man inside. I restrained Jerry from following him in. When Thomas emerged, looking relieved and fumbling his fly buttons, we hauled him back upstairs to his proprietors and hurried up to the balcony where Jane had saved us seats.

An untidy little procession was making its way down the left aisle toward the stage, with Thomas clipped between Les Burgevin and Larry Wallis, who appeared to be trying to support him with their bodies without actually laying hands on him. With discreet bits of pushing and hauling they got him up the stairs to the stage and guided him to a chair at left rear. As Burgevin scurried through a formal introduction, broken by troubled glances over his shoulder at his problem, the audience waited tensely for the event to define itself as tragedy or comedy.

Swiveling about on his hard seat like a dying top, Thomas pawed at the contents of a flat leather envelope, from which he had taken not books but what looked like a hundred or so rumpled yellow second sheets which he now shuffled aimlessly, his hands apparently unrelated to his eyes. I sat with my whole hide prickling, feeling a weird mixture of sympathy and revulsion, afraid to speak lest it come out as a sob or a guffaw. It seemed hopeless to suppose that the reeling wretched body and those wandering unfocused eyes could produce an hour's coherent function. Mostly I wished that a curtain might be drawn and the man taken off and put to bed. Yet Thomas survived the lonely walk to the front, deposited his fan of yellow sheets, and stood holding the lectern with his left hand while his body pivoted slowly on the fulcrum of his right heel.

Always ready, Nemesis struck hard. One could feel Thomas's parching gullet in one's own throat. A pitcher and a glass had been placed on the side apron of the lectern, and he swung the pitcher up and over the glass with a brave florid gesture. Everyone else saw at once what Thomas could not see at all: whoever supplied the utensils had forgotten to fill the pitcher. He held it aloft for a long agonizing minute, in a pouring posture, as the cogs of his alcoholic brain struggled to mesh on the fact that there really wasn't any water there. To their honor the audience kept silent—as I remember it, not a single titter. Les Burgevin rushed down, took the pitcher, and went out with it, and while we all waited Thomas stood planted on flat feet, braced with both hands on the lectern, facing the audience with desperate goggling eyes, now and again detaching a hand to poke indecisively at his ragged pile of yellow paper. It was still impossible to believe that he could find what he was looking for, or even know what he wanted to find, or read it if he found it.

When he began to read the miracle was immediate and complete. Out of that ugly disordered body proceeded what seemed the world's most beautiful speaking voice, perfectly controlled, in flawless performance. In form, content, and execution our anticipated farce had turned into something grand and astonishing. We had supposed that Thomas, if he did not simply collapse, if he could read at all, would read a selection of his own poems in the common way of performing poets. In fact he read few works of his own; I recall only "Fern Hill," his paean to country childhood, "green and dying," and "After the Funeral (In Memory of Ann Jones)," his elegy for "dead, humped Ann." Nine-tenths of what he read was work of late Victorian, Edwardian, and Georgian poets, most of it not very familiar, poems of strong feeling and traditional forms; and his magnificent voice made them seem luminous and exalted. I remember in particular a lot of Thomas Hardy, and remember the dawn of the revelation that this was a very great poet indeed.

This reticence in advancing his own claims, this generosity to the recent dead, was a part of what was most moving about Thomas's performance. He was celebrating not the ego but poetry itself, the art, the general patrimony. His reading said simply: these are things I love and wish to preserve and present. The rest of the grandeur of the day lay in the performance, though I don't like to use the word—Thomas seemed so little to perform. The fumbling fingers always found the right sheet, the drowned eyes and the drowned brain somehow managed to come to bear—perfectly. There was no backing and filling, never a stumble, never a hesitation, not so much as a slurred syllable. I had never heard poetry, never heard anything, read so beautifully. Poetry's old claims to be an oral art suddenly made complete sense: Thomas embodied the function—*vates*, scop, bard. His voice rolled and rang with the resonance and clarity of a deep-tongued bell, perfect in pitch, modulation, articulation. Yet Thomas hardly seemed to be playing, not really performing at all. He applied a gift, as it were anonymously, to certain beautiful forms that an art had taken. And all the time one was thinking that this prodigally gifted man was killing himself, that he could not live long as he was living.

A few of us gathered about Thomas in the road outside after the reading, and he seemed little clearer in his head than when he arrived. Peter Viereck was in the group, and he introduced himself as well as one could, mentioning as identification that he had recently brought out a book called *Conservatism Revisited*. "Don' wanna revisi' conserv'tism," Thomas mumbled, and on that note we parted. Next day we heard tales of the poet playing Priapus in the shrubbery about the dormitories and expressing leering admiration for the golden bosoms of elderly spinsters of the English department, before he finally collapsed facedown across a table full of drinks.

I had driven home in a state of complex and qualified exhilaration. In my excitement I sat down and wrote a poem about the experience, finished in a single sitting except for bits of tinkering over the next few days. Eventually it was published in an obscure magazine, but I haven't wanted to get it out and reread it, for I know I would find it sentimental and overstated. It began rhetorically, I remember, "You, sir, are the thing itself." In my first optimism I sent the poem to one of the best of the literary quarterlies, and the editors returned it with a note saying that Dylan Thomas had been on their campus and they had not thought him so—not the thing itself. But I still feel my judgment as accurate for the occasion described. What I had tried to express was the extraordinary mixture of pity, disgust, and enchantment one felt in the event, the way the performance had soared above the stink of conduct and perhaps of character, the power of art to have its way.

It was not so much that one had seen Shelley plain, though it was something like that. The vulgarity, the self-indulgence, the latent charlatanism were too obvious and awful. Yet most curious of all was the way both the sins and the glories of the event turned impersonal, detaching themselves from the man and attaching themselves to the function. I found, for example, that I could not even think of Thomas's triumphant reading as an act of personal courage. It did not seem conscious enough for that, not sufficiently willed. It was as if there were a set of switches inside the hulk too deep for the booze to reach, attached to instincts that he housed but did not control. The instincts to survive, to speak, to praise poetry tripped their own switches and performed.

I have been struggling again to describe an intense experience in the arts, and I suppose I have overstated it again. When the exhilaration had died down one was left feeling mainly desolation and pity at the visible self-destruction of a splendid talent: the sense of waste that A. C. Bradley identifies with tragedy. But that is a big word, probably too big.

II

After six pleasant years at Sweet Briar College in Virginia, I was again offered a position at Mount Holyoke in the fall of 1957, and we decided to return to New England. I suppose it was because I was teaching the course in contemporary poetry that I was assigned the honor of fetching Robert Frost the ten miles from Amherst for his reading in South Hadley in October 1962. The college was celebrating its 125th anniversary, and Frost's appearance was one of the major events. Jane naturally wanted to share the wealth, so she went along for the trip. Frost was living, as was his habit in the periods he spent at Amherst College, in the Lord Jeffrey Amherst, a homely-elegant fake-old inn just off the town green and the college campus. I inquired at the desk and was directed up the plain wide central stairway to a room at the head of the stairs. I knew, of course, that Frost was an old man of eighty-seven, reputed to be fairly salty, and one was familiar with photographs of his seamed Cro-Magnon face under a cap of white hair. That is what I saw when he answered my knock, with a glance from under out of bright blue, slightly wary eyes and a noncommittal smile. As he moved about the room collecting his books and papers, his countryman's sturdy body was stooped but brisk and efficient. It was obvious that this old party was very much at himself.

In the car heading back over the Notch to South Hadley we chatted quietly and comfortably, all of us friendly and unrestrained, Frost often turning in his seat to speak directly to Jane in the back. She and I had been rereading the *Collected Poems* in anticipation of the evening, and Frost took obvious pleasure in the pleasure Jane expressed in "The Need of Being Versed in Country Things." It was a clear, quiet, cool evening with a beautiful full moon. I had tried to time the trip to allow Frost a few minutes to relax before he went on stage, and we actually reached town with fifteen or twenty minutes in hand. A local poet had asked me, however, to tell Frost that he wished to speak with him privately, before the reading if possible, and I had promised to deliver the message. Now, when I did so, the old man said at once: "Let's go look at the moon." And that is just what we did, driving a couple of miles to Cold Hill over the line in Granby, where we parked facing the full moon in a clear sky and talked peacefully for another ten minutes. Let me say, lest you miss it, that that quiet chat was the crown of the evening for us.

Chapin Auditorium was packed, balconies and all. Frost read, or, as he preferred to put it, "said" his poems in a New Englander's strong monotone, rather dry and flat, and varied only by his hard-shell commentary around the edges. He took an obvious, and obviously deep-seated, pleasure in his old curmudgeon, wicked conservative's role, and he chose to read far too many of his little dogmatical apothegms. Still there were enough of the great old lyrics to reassure one that this was a great poet when he wasn't posing; and as an addendum at the end he took time to read the poem Jane had admired. When he said, "One had to be versed in country things / Not to believe the phoebes wept," I found my own eyes suddenly prickling.

III

When it dawned on me that at long last I was in a fair way to qualify for an academic sabbatical, I began thinking about a big task to occupy it, and in 1960 I started poking into the subject of John Quinn. My interest in Quinn went all the way back to college days, when I had first noticed how many capital works of modern painting and sculpture had been owned by him; later in reading in and about Joyce and Yeats and Pound and Eliot I kept finding his tracks in their lives as well. It struck me that this Irish-American lawyer and universal midwife to modernism in the arts was a phenomenon that needed explaining, and I resolved then that when I got some free time I would have a go at it. Now I read Jeanne Robert Foster's transcripts of a big selection of Quinn's correspondence in the New York Public Library, and soon I met Mrs. Foster herself, living in elderly retirement in Schenectady; then I met Quinn's heirs, Mary and Frank Conroy, in California. All gave me their blessing and friendly assistance, and my way was cleared.

Quinn having died in 1924, the survivors among his friends and beneficiaries were growing few. I began at once to write to those I knew of, beginning with Eliot and Pound. Joyce and Yeats were long gone, but I wrote to Mrs. Yeats, the famous "George," who had known Quinn herself. She never replied, though ultimately I did manage to corner her for an interview in Dublin. Pound was back in Europe after his release from St. Elizabeth's in Washington, where he had been sent as "insane" following his trial for wartime treason. He too ignored my letters, but after a bit I had a note from Dorothy Pound urging me to persevere in seeing Ezra no matter how he behaved. Eliot answered promptly and sweetly: he had never known Quinn in the flesh but he remembered his help gratefully and would be willing to talk about his long-distance experience of the man.

Jane and I were excited and happy at the thought of a year of freedom abroad, for we had always lived humbly and parochially and at forty-five had never set foot outside the United States except for a few hours in places like Tijuana and Montreal. As my Fulbright research fellowship attached me loosely to University College London, our base was to be England and particularly London. We thought our tastes and the school needs of our son, Colin, then nearing eleven, called for something of the village or suburban order, and we soon found a "semidetached" half of a house in Walton-on-Thames in Surrey, thirty minutes by train to Waterloo Station.

My official justification for coming abroad was the need to interview surviving associates of Quinn before they died or, if they had already slipped over, to interview their heirs or other descendants. I was trying, of course, to draw as near as possible to my subject as a living man, and also pursuing my minimal practical need for permissions to quote from the many letters to Quinn from major artists and writers of the first quarter of the century. Most of my quarry were in England and Ireland, but Pound was in Italy and there was a scattering in France. My prize objectives were undoubtedly Pound, Eliot, Mrs. Yeats, and Picasso if I could pin him down (I never did). I hoped to arrange my traveling so that the whole family could enjoy it, and that meant that it had to fit into Colin's school holidays. In point of fact there were comparatively few people living whom I could hope to see, and as most of my requests in regard to Quinn's correspondence could be handled by letter, the whole process required only a small fraction of my time. In the upshot I spent three-quarters of my free year turning the notes and papers I had already collected into a preliminary manuscript of four hundred pages, and worked at critical essays on other subjects I had stored up.

As a Londoner, T. S. Eliot should have been the most accessible of my people, but that did not prove to be the case. When I wrote him first in the fall, his secretary at Faber and Faber replied that he was ill. When I wrote again after a decent interval, I was told that he had gone to warmer parts for an extended rest. My next letter brought a reply that Mr. Eliot was back in London, but now the "lift" at Faber's was out of order and he could not get into his office. By this time it was early spring of 1964 and I was feeling distinctly evaded. But I kept on with my politely pressing notes, and I was finally assigned an appointment for an afternoon toward the end of April.

I had been in correspondence with a young man from Virginia who was trying to trace the history of the manuscript of *The Waste Land*, the famous original with Ezra Pound's cuts and emendations; and of course I was interested in that matter myself and meant to make it one object of our talk to see whether Eliot could or would shed any light. That Quinn had owned the manuscript was common knowledge, but it had dropped from sight after his death in 1924 and was generally supposed to have been destroyed or otherwise lost.

When I presented myself at the Faber headquarters, a high red-brick structure in the style of a Queen Anne townhouse at the corner of Russell Square, the receptionist told me that Mr. Eliot had not yet arrived but that Mrs. Eliot had telephoned to say he would be along shortly. I waited in a room off the central hallway, admiring the elegant plainness of the room pilastered with glass-enclosed cases of Faber and Faber books, according to the self-contemplative or onanistic habit of publishers. After a quarter of an hour I saw T. S. Eliot pass my doorway, stumping briskly across the lobby toward the famous lift, bent almost double over his umbrella-cane. I was prepared for the fact that Eliot at seventy-five would not be the Arrow Collar dandy of his early pictures, nor yet the wise tortoise of his middle years; but this ailing old gentleman, thin and excessively stooped, was still a shock. Meeting him on the street, in his dark suit and long coat, with his intent straight-ahead look out of the pale face under the black City hat, one would have taken him for the classical type of the crotchety old London clubman in a no-nonsense mood. Eliot looked frail but plenty formidable.

I waited peacefully to be called, and in a few minutes Eliot's secretary came to fetch me. Letters from this personage had always been signed "M. I. Drage," as I remember the name, and I expected to see some sort of male; but Drage turned out to be a quietly stylish young woman, tallish, graceful, softly tailored, very pretty in a bluestocking way. These Fabers had a great sense of ensemble. I ogled her as well as I could in the bad light of the lift as we rode upward, chatting about our sizable correspondence.

With a quiet, wary politeness Eliot welcomed me into his office, or his "room," as the English say. It was situated at the very top of the house under the eaves, on what must have been the fourth or fifth floor, a room longish and rather narrow, lined with shelves and lit by dormer windows opposite the door. It looked like a place where one man had lived for a long time and done a lot of work. The general effect was plain but not bare or tasteless. The light painted walls and the tops of bookcases were lined with many framed photographs, of groups and single figures, some familiar to me, others mysterious.

The truth was that Eliot and I did not have a great deal to say to each other, so long as our subject was to be John Quinn. He agreed with me that Quinn deserved and needed a biography—if the medium was not sinful in itself, as I rather suspected Eliot suspected, with his instinct for privacy. He clearly wished to help, but his capacity was limited by the fact that their relationship had been conducted entirely by mail or by third parties, particularly Ezra Pound, the universal middleman. He spoke warmly of Quinn's general helpfulness to the modern movement in the arts, his court defense of *Ulysses,* his work for the American publication of Joyce and Pound, and especially of Quinn's management of Eliot's own early poems, most notably the publication of *The Waste Land* in 1922 and the Dial Prize of $2,000. He proved as anxious as I was to discuss the missing manuscript; but, far from shedding light on the mystery, he wanted to know what light I could shed. When I told him that I had found no trace of the manuscript, he threw up his hands and said gloomily: "It must have been destroyed." His concern, he said, was chiefly on Pound's behalf: he wanted the manuscript recovered as a record of his friend's critical and editorial genius.

On one detail of the history I was able to straighten Eliot out. His recollection was that he had sold the manuscript of the long poem to Quinn; but I knew from studying the old letters between them that the case had been a bit different. I explained that what had happened, forty years earlier, was that in gratitude for Quinn's good offices Eliot had pressed him to accept the manuscript as a gift; but Quinn, who knew, mainly from Pound, of Eliot's general neediness, had insisted that he must pay for the manuscript. Eliot, still wishing to make a gift and feeling that Quinn perhaps secretly preferred his earlier work, then proposed to send all that he had preserved of his early drafts and typescripts. Quinn wrote him to send the lot: he would accept the *Waste Land* manuscript as a present, on condition that Eliot allow him to pay for the other matter at a figure to be set by an appraiser. In the long run Quinn got early in 1923 *The Waste Land* plus some sixty pages of drafts of poems, including a workbook dating back to 1909, for which he sent Eliot a check for $140, having added $20 to the appraised value. Eliot had expressed himself at the time as well content, and he was not in the least resentful now, except that he felt baffled and gloomy about the subsequent vanishing of the *Waste Land* manuscript. He wanted to find the manuscript, or, failing that, at least to understand what had happened to it and perhaps to identify somebody to blame. But I could not help him.

We went on to talk in general terms of Eliot's letters to Quinn, and I put to him my request to be allowed to quote from the letters in my biography. I could assure him that they did him nothing but honor: they showed a hard-pressed young man, serious, intelligent, and scrupulous, struggling without self-pity against severe constraints to shape a career as a poet and man of letters. But Eliot required to see the letters before committing himself, and I promised to send him copies. I supposed that he wanted to recover the letters for natural future uses of his own. We talked also of Pound's wonderfully ebullient letters to Quinn, and the contrasting silence I had met in attempts to reach him. Elliot had had a characteristic postcard from Pound recently, and he advised me to keep trying. It was clear that he kept his warm personal affection for Pound.

Beyond that point our talk was desultory and not long, and when things lagged I questioned him about one or another of the many photographs in the room, including that of Groucho Marx—a good friend, Eliot said. But when I identified another picture as John Lehmann, he flared up angrily: it was not Lehmann and he wanted no pictures of Lehmann. I had blundered onto a sore nerve of some sort. I stayed enough longer to soothe him down, but we had used up our usefulness to each other, and I soon took my leave.

Perhaps the time has come to tell the story of what I later learned about the history of the *Waste Land* manuscript and to describe my small part in that mystery. It was not till a year or so after Eliot's death in 1965 that I learned that the manuscript had indeed survived, and in a perfectly appropriate place, the Berg Collection in the New York Public Library. Mary Conroy telephoned me one night long after I had gone back to work at Mount Holyoke, to say that she had had qualms of conscience about concealing from me the fact that she had sold the manuscript to the Berg Collection in 1958—under a vow of secrecy to the library, which she had always strictly observed. She had now told the people at the library that she felt obliged to confide in me, swearing me to keep the secret in turn. I was fascinated, of course, but frustrated by the imposed conditions, and angry on Eliot's behalf that he had been allowed to die in ignorance of the fate of his treasure.

The library people had had their own reasons for the hugger-mugger, which it is not my business to explain. They now decided, in any case, that the time had come to show their hand. John Quinn's immense, varied, and valuable correspondence was in the process of passing into their possession as a gift from his heirs. They planned to honor the gift by unveiling a carved inscription to Quinn, and to mount in the Berg Collection a big exhibition of star items from the Quinn papers, with the manuscript of *The Waste Land* as the pièce de résistance. These events were timed to coincide with the publication of my biography of Quinn in the first week of November 1968, and on a day of dismal fall rain they all duly occurred. T. S. Eliot's lost manuscript lay mummy-fashion in a locked glass case near the door of the Berg Collection, with its top page not quite legible under a sheet of gauze. That was the first and last time I saw the manuscript.

The resurrection naturally attracted a lot of attention among people who care about such things, and its appearance at the same time as my book seemed to imply an occult relationship. The manuscript was featured in press accounts of the Quinn exhibition, which generally managed to suggest that the document had been hidden away for my benefit as Quinn's biographer—that in effect I had sat on it for years, keeping Eliot and other legitimately interested persons in ignorance, while I mined it for my own purposes. Having had nothing to do with the long history of the scheme, and having in fact never laid eyes on the document itself, I felt the unfairness of the imputation. Yet I felt that I could not clear myself, and set the scholarly record straight, without radically embarrassing the principals, who had been otherwise kind and generous to me. So I thought I could only keep the public peace, and I have done so for ten years; but most of those I was concerned to protect are dead now, like the issue itself, and I am relieved to be able to clean the slate.

IV

We used Colin's Easter holiday in a trip to Dublin and the west of Ireland, and I did accomplish an interview with Mrs. Yeats, who turned out to answer the telephone if not letters, and who proved toothless and utterly charming. Then we spent Colin's Whitsun week in Paris, where the functional highlights were a meeting with the widow of Henri-Pierre Roche (whom Leo Stein called "The Great Introducer" and who had been Quinn's chief agent in buying modern French paintings and sculpture) and a view of Quinn's splendid bequest to the French nation, *Le Cirque* by Georges Seurat, anonymously and insultingly labeled in the Jeu de Paume as the gift of "an American." We stayed on in Walton through July and planned to invest what little money and time we had left on a second trip to the continent, where our objectives would be Ezra Pound and a hurried look at general culture.

I continued to write to Pound and to dream of an answer. At last Mrs. Pound wrote that he would be at 131 Sant' Ambrogio in Rapallo during our interval, and she advised me to see him and take my chances. She said that he had been ill, had undergone an operation, was in an unpredictable frame of mind, and "hardly ever bothers to speak." But if I went prepared with definite questions he might be inclined to help out. I wrote him once more to say I would be appearing and named an actual day. We loaded our little MG sedan onto the channel steamer and drove south through Switzerland and the Alps into northern Italy. We passed a few happy days in Venice, then Florence, then Rome, and then headed back north along the coast toward Rapallo, stopping all too briefly at places like Siena and Orvieto.

Of course everything in Europe was new to us, and my only impressions of Rapallo had come from scrappy references in Pound's published letters and in the antic introductory matter of Yeats's mad book *A Vision*, which had led me to expect something small and unspoiled, primitive-Renaissance. So the jumbled busy modern town was a disappointment, though its situation remained beautiful, with the greeny-brown hilly landscape rolling down to a roomy Mediterranean bay. We arrived in the early evening of the day preceding the one I had named to Pound and found beds in a small hotel in the center of town. After dinner I set about finding directions for the morrow. I began with the telephone book, remembering my luck with Mrs. Yeats, but there was no listing for Ezra Pound. I had assumed that he would be a well-known local character, but nobody in the hotel or its neighborhood seemed to have heard of him. Evidently his absence in America following his wartime troubles had been long enough to blot him from local memory. The best people could do was to point me vaguely in the direction of Sant' Ambrogio. My inquiries were made halting and inconclusive by my impressionistic Italian, limited to a few nouns and adjectives. The desk clerk at the hotel advised me to leave the task of finding Pound to a taxi driver next morning. That seemed to make sense, and I went quietly to bed, feeling uncharacteristically optimistic: I would find Ezra Pound, he would be glad to see me, and we would have a long rich talk about John Quinn.

Our August weather had been hot and dry all through Italy, and the following morning produced a blazing sun in a clear sky. By the time we had finished breakfast the temperature was in the nineties and climbing. I found a taxi and gave the driver the card on which I had carefully printed Pound's name and address. He accepted it with an air of cheery intelligence, and we set out. But soon we stopped, and he appeared to be asking directions of a woman trudging along the road. She shrugged and walked on. We proceeded, in a tentative sort of way, and the driver stopped and talked with the next pedestrian, with the same apparent result. The driver and I now got out and stood in the road while he tried, for the most part manually, to explain the problem. Sant' Ambrogio was not a street, as I had supposed, but a mountain—the big low mountain that lay behind the whole town of Rapallo. We were standing in fact at the base of it, and looking above I could see that the terrain was rambled over by an unsystematic system of narrow curving and climbing roads, along which dozens of villas were dotted at irregular intervals. Moreover the houses were not numbered according to sequence or proximity but according to some unreason that seemed to be pure whim, or perhaps the order of composition. Number 40 was just as likely to be next to Number 12 as next to Number 39. Nobody had ever heard of Signor Pound, or could point to Number 131. Apparently one had to live there to know where it was. We could only fly blind, and we did that for the better part of an hour, poking about the lower slopes, scanning numbers, while I questioned everyone we saw in my kindergarten vocabulary: *poeta, Americano, vecchio, barba,* and so on.

Finally, thwarted and angry and wondering how long my stock of lire could satisfy the ticking meter, I decided to dismiss my driver and take up the quest on foot—it couldn't be much worse that way. But I hadn't reckoned with the heat. I toiled on uphill like a sweaty St. Francis, inquiring as I went, while my shirt soaked through and damp arcs moved down the front and back of my trousers. For years afterward I wore that shirt for outdoor work, with its dark ring about the waist where my leather belt had faded. At last, dripping wet but no wiser with noon approaching, I struggled out onto a sort of plateau on top of the mountain. I was surprised to see a little low *bodega,* and it looked mighty good: at least I could sit down and drink a cold beer. This I did, in the cool dark interior amid a small crowd of native proletarians quite unflurried by my arrival. It occurred to me that I might as well try my Ezra Pound card on the bartender. I did so, and the necessary miracle occurred. Of course he knew Signor Pound! His face lit up in a big smile, he tossed a phrase to his clients who beamed and chattered Italian. Everybody knew Signor Pound. He lived nearby. Furthermore Giorgio there was about to walk that way and would be charmed to guide me.

I followed the brisk chunky figure, a New York bricklayer's figure, across the dry brown hilltop for a couple of hundred yards until he pointed me with a beautiful gesture to a modest two-story white stuccoed house. The doorway bore the improbable number: 131. I took a deep breath and knocked. The door was opened by a pretty elderly lady with white hair and a round face with a serene smile. "Mrs. Pound?" I inquired. "No," she said sweetly, "Olga Rudge." Mine not to reason why. I identified myself and my errand briefly and said that I had written Mr. Pound that I would appear that day. Mr. Pound was resting, she said, but she would inquire. Waiting and trepidating on the doorstep, I racked my brain for Olga Rudge and found her dimly among Pound's early letters: a musician from Ohio, one of those Europeanized Americans of the great expatriate generation. It was not till several years later that I got her straight as Ezra Pound's longtime alternative wife and the mother of one of his children.

In a minute she returned: Pound would see me. She led me up a narrow stairway to a small room off a hallway. I remember the room as completely white and almost completely bare, a monk's cell with unadorned plaster walls: a scene that Giotto or Piero della Francesca could have painted with easy familiarity. The poet was stretched out on his back on one of the few bits of furniture, a sort of raised pallet, a rude, very narrow bed against the wall. Except for his eyes he too was all white, white as the walls, white cotton shirt and trousers, marble-white face, hands, and bare feet, snow-white hair and eyebrows and short beard. The eyes were a vivid blue, not an old man's bleary blue but bright and light, a boy's aquamarine. His body looked terribly frail and thin, corpse-thin. Except for the eyes, he looked like a man who might die within the hour. I felt the grossness of my intrusion, but what could I do but pronounce my name and my purpose once more? He shot a blue-lightning glance at me from under the white brows, swung his feet to the floor, smiled and shook my hand, and said nothing.

Miss Rudge led us to an adjoining room, a sort of study, almost as white and even more bright but less bare, where there were tables and chairs, plain and modern. She proposed a drink, and I said I would be pleased to have anything cool. While she was gone I chatted a bit hectically at Pound, who smiled tranquilly and said nothing. In a minute she returned with a tray of glasses and a flagon of chilled white wine, very dry and delicious to my palate, parched by my hot climb and now by nervousness. There then ensued one of the strangest hours of my life.

After a few minutes of polite talk with Miss Rudge I showed my sheet of questions to Ezra Pound, and he nodded approvingly. I put my first question and sat with my notebook and ballpoint poised. Pound looked intelligent and said nothing. I sat quietly, giving him what I supposed he wanted, time to think. When nothing had come after a couple of minutes, I thought perhaps I should try another question. After another two-minute silence I tried a third question. Same result. I chatted a bit more with Miss Rudge. She topped up our wineglasses. I directed a fourth question to Pound. Silence. I tried my second question again. Intelligent-looking silence. I began talking of what I knew of the subjects I had advanced, hoping to start a flow of reminiscence about the things I knew Pound and Quinn had worked at together—of *The Waste Land* and the *Cantos*, of Epstein and Gaudier-Brzeska and Wyndham Lewis, of W. B. Yeats and his artist father, of Margaret Anderson and *Ulysses* and the *Little Review*. Nothing came. I described my interviews with T. S. Eliot and Mrs. Yeats. Pound nodded brightly and silently.

So it went on. Miss Rudge was serene and friendly, but she made no reference to Pound's silence and did not encourage him to speak. She and I talked of Quinn, and of life and letters generally, and Pound listened and occasionally sipped his wine. Every so often I made another hesitant dart at him with a new question, or an old one repeated. As far as I could tell he followed me perfectly well, and I thought he seemed interested in my enterprise and felt sympathetic, even approving; but he had no intention of speaking. His eyes would light up, his mouth would open, occasionally his lips would even move. But no sound emerged. After a time it all became too absurd and painful. I couldn't tell who was torturing whom, or why, but I felt tortured. Finally I stood up to go, and I asked a last desperate question: "Is a biography of John Quinn a thing worth doing?" Then it happened. "S-S-Certainly," he said, in a sort of emphatic whisper. I could no longer say that Ezra Pound had refused to speak to me. But that was the only word I was ever to get out of him, spoken or written. Even my standard request to be allowed to quote from his letters had finally to be granted by James Laughlin of New Directions, acting as a guardian of Pound's literary affairs.

Miss Rudge was walking down into the town to do some shopping, and she offered to show me the short way down the mountain. As we walked we naturally talked about the morning's performance. She obviously felt sorry for me, but she was not in the least apologetic. Pound's condition was quite unpredictable, she said, and she knew no way to explain it. Some days he was full of life—walked down to the town and swam in the bay, worked at his poems, made recordings, talked on the radio. Other days he retreated into the Great Muteness. Nobody could say when or why. I had struck one of the silent days.

My state of mind, as we walked and thenceforward, was rueful and confused—and amused. Fundamentally I felt the Pound episode as comic. I had traveled from top to bottom of Europe to interrogate the Great Apparition, in Emerson's phrase, and it had answered me with a single word. Rather like *Peer Gynt*, I suppose. On the other hand I could not honestly say I had been had. Pound had never encouraged me to come. I had more or less forced myself upon him, having chosen to disregard the signal of his disregarding my letters. I couldn't say whether he could not or would not talk, whether he actually willed his silence; all I knew was that he didn't talk. Perhaps he had had enough of what Henry James's old lady called the "publishing scoundrel"—diggers like me, mining his genius and the history of his hard work. Yet I had never felt, during that weird abortive interrogation, that he was scorning me or my purpose. I had arrived on a day he had devoted to silence. And in spite of my frustration I had found the hour deeply moving. He was a beautiful old man, I did know what he had written and what he had done, good and bad, I had seen the bright blue eyes and the lips moving. The one word they had chosen to pronounce was a good word. I was not satisfied, but I had been rewarded.

Death of the Artist
In Memoriam, Henry Rox

I

His heart had told him twice to write his will
and stop his work, but neither had he done;
free of his task at last, old age begun,
he found no time to waste in being ill.
He had new tricks to try in fire and steel
picked up from the bright young man coming on:
the batwing wood madonnas are all gone,
the harp-strung terra-cotta men rest well.

Too stiff and still all that, though well enough.
Now his tightrope artist swaggers and flings
his parasol, tips from a toe in space;
his little metal girl is made of stuff
hard in itself, but her wire bouquet rings
like bluebells, a spring of springs, a grace of grace.

II

He made a little woman all of springs
hung by one elastic arm from a wire,
navel to crotch a long live *mons* like fire,
lovely coiled breasts tangled in her rib rings.
The one he'd wed and loved above all things
year after year sat frozen on her pyre
of pain, mute except for her pitiful quire
for scrawls and her laugh at whatever brings.

So, stone limbed and steel spirited, she loved.
His chisel rattled on the floor and then
his bones. Within she heard and would have moved.
All night she feared. Next day when friends looked in
she wrote, "I think he's dead"; and so it proved:
dead and colder than she had ever been.

INDEX

Adams, Charles Francis, 76
Adams, Henry (*The Education of Henry Adams*): its stature, 65, 66; pose of failure, 65, 66, 70, 74, 78–79; its history, 65, 66, 70, 76; its structure, 66, 68, 70, 75, 76, 78–79, 80; and *Mont Saint Michel and Chartres*, 66, 68, 70, 86; elegiac motive, 66, 68, 71, 87; its models (Benjamin Franklin, Saint Augustine, Jean-Jacques Rousseau), 67; artistic ambition, 67, 68; self-distancing devices, 67, 71; atmosphere, background, 69; New England sensibility, 72, 73; life as game, 72, 74; definition of education, 75, 77, 78, 79, 82; "The Dynamo and the Virgin," 81–86
Adams, John, 72
Adams, John Quincy, 72
Adams, Marian Hooper, 76, 77, 78, 79
Auden, W. H., 7, 90

Barber, Francis, 44
Blotner, Joseph: *Faulkner*, 1
Boswell, Sir Alexander, Lord Auchinleck, 9, 11, 13, 17
Boswell, James: *Boswell's London Journal*, 9–16 *passim*; mentors, 17; *Journal of a Tour to the Hebrides*, 20–22; dissipations, 24–26, 27; *The Life of Samuel Johnson*, 15–16, 19, 22–23, 32
Boswell, Margaret, 9
Bradley, A. C., 45, 146
Brawne, Fanny, 47
Burke, Edmund, 30, 44
Burke, Richard, 42
Byron, George, Lord, 48

Casement, Sir Roger, 5–6

Dalrymple, Sir David, 8, 10, 13

Eliot, T. S., 7, 89–90, 148, 149–50; *The Waste Land*, 149, 151, 152–53

Frost, Robert, 147–48

Garrick, David, 33

Gaskell, Charles Milnes, 66–67
Goldsmith, Oliver, 12, 41
Gonne, Maud, 93, 95
Gosse, Edmund: *Father and Son*, 7
Gregory, Lady Augusta, 92, 96, 102

Hay, John, 66, 76, 79, 88

James, Henry, 65, 68, 72, 158
James, William, 65, 68
Johnson, Samuel: *London: A Poem*, 15; letters to Boswell, 18, 20, 22–24, 27–28; *Journey to the Western Islands of Scotland*, 21; *The Rambler*, 31; his "seraglio," 32–33, 41; *Life of Savage*, 33; *Lives of the Poets*, 33, 41; *English Dictionary*, 33–34; *Prayers and Meditations*, 34–35
Joyce, James: *Ulysses*, 3, 18, 151

Keats, George and Georgiana: John Keats's letters to, 46–57 *passim*
Keats, John: letters, 3, 7, 46–57
—Works: "La Belle Dame sans Merci," 53; *Endymion*, 46, 57; "The Eve of Saint Agnes," 47; "Hyperion," 46; "Ode on a Grecian urn," 49, 57, 58, 59–60; "Ode on Indolence," 49, 57, 58; "Ode on Melancholy," 57, 58; "Ode to a Nightingale," 52, 56, 57, 58–59; "Ode to Psyche," 46, 53, 57, 58; "To Autumn," 49, 57, 58, 60–63; "To Sleep," 55; "Why Did I Laugh Tonight?" 52
Keats, Tom, 47
King, Clarence, 75, 76, 81, 88

La Farge, John, 78, 85

Melville, Herman, 3, 35, 83

O'Connor, Frank, 89; *An Only Child*, 126; compared with V. S. Pritchett, 126–28; the family, 128–31, 136–37, 139–40; education, 131–34, 137; "Judas," 134; "The Procession of Life," 134; civil war, 134–36; "Guests of the Nation," 135; *My Father's Son*, 137; Lennox Robinson,

137, 140, 141; Geoffrey Phibbs, 137–38; George William Russell, 138; William Butler Yeats, 138, 140–41

Pound, Ezra, 6, 94, 95–96, 148, 149, 151–52, 153–58

Pritchett, V. S.: compared with Frank O'Connor, 107, 109, 118, 125; the Pritchett family, 107, 111–12, 122–24, 127–28; education, 110; Christian Science, 108, 114, 115, 117, 118–20; *A Cab at the Door*, 108, 111–12, 115; *Midnight Oil*, 107, 112–13, 127–28; France, 113; Ireland, 116–18; Spain, 118–19, 121, 127

Quinn, John, 3–5, 148, 149, 150–51, 152–53

Reynolds, Sir Joshua, 17, 30
Roché, Henri-Pierre, 153
Rox, Henry, 159–60

Shakespeare, William: Keats's love for, 45, 48, 54, 56; *King Lear*, 45, 54, 56

Shelley, Percy Bysshe, 57

Tennyson, Alfred, Lord, 1
Thomas, Dylan, 143–46
Thrale, Mrs. Hester Lynch, 17, 29
Trilling, Lionel, 45*n*, 51

Wilkes, John, 10

Yeats, "George," 95, 148, 153
Yeats, William Butler: Yeats and Pollexfen families, 89, 90–93, 106; Riversdale, 102
—Works: "An Acre of Grass," 103; *Autobiography*, 7, 91; "Easter 1916," 90; "Ego Dominus Tuus," 92; "The Gyres," 104; "High Talk," 104–5; "In Memory of Major Robert Gregory," 90; "Introductory Rhymes" to *Responsibilities*, 90–92; "Lapis Lazuli," 104, 141; "Meditations in Time of Civil War," 97; "The Municipal Gallery Revisited," 100–101; "The Tower," 96–100; "Under Ben Bulben," 106; *A Vision*, 95

WITHDRAWN from the Alma College Library